The Sociopath Next Door

the sociopath next door

The Ruthless Versus the Rest of Us

Martha Stout, Ph.D.

BROADWAY BOOKS NEW YORK

PRINTED IN THE UNITED STATES OF AMERICA

Visit our website at www.broadwaybooks.com

First edition published 2005

Book design by Ellen Cipriano

Library of Congress Cataloging-in-Publication Data
Stout, Martha, 1953–
The sociopath next door : the ruthless versus the rest of us / Martha Stout—1st ed.
p. cm.
1. Psychopaths. 2. Antisocial personality disorders. I. Title.

RC555.S76 2004
616.85'82—dc22
2004051874

ISBN 0-7679-1581-X

3 5 7 9 10 8 6 4 2

For Steve Stout,
my brother and the person I think of first
when I think of strength of character

The conscience of a people is their power.

—John Dryden

contents

acknowledgments

Much of the time, the absorbing task of writing a book feels less like authoring and more like channeling, through your fingers and a keyboard, the lessons and inspiration of countless other people, wise friends known over many years and teachers disguised as students, patients, and colleagues. I wish I could go back in time and thank them all, and I take delight in this chance to thank the people who most helped and supported me during the year I wrote *The Sociopath Next Door.*

For her commentary and utter indispensability, and her patience, I thank my friend and colleague Carol Kauffman, she of the legendary creativity at solving problems, whose generosity never skipped a beat, even though she was in the middle of writing *Pivot Points.*

Because none of this would have been possible without her moving commitment to her mission, and for her having been always a deep well of grace, comprehension, and heart in a wide desert, I thank my agent and treasured friend, Susan Lee Cohen.

If I had attempted to design the world's most superb editor, I could not have done nearly so well as Kristine Puopolo at Broadway Books, and I thank her for her intelligence, her precision, and her extraordinary ability to be quietly right, always, without ever being intrusive.

I thank Diane Wemyss for her caring and her organizing, and for having suggested one of the events I write about, and Elizabeth Haymaker for her charm across the miles.

I thank Steve Stout and Darcy Wakefield, for making me believe in love again.

Once again—and always—I thank my remarkable parents, Eva Deaton Stout and Adrian Phillip Stout, for showing me just how much love and light two people of surpassing conscience can bring to the world.

And with awe, and more love than I could have imagined before I knew her, I would like to thank my daughter, Amanda, my first reader and my most insightful one. She has taught me, among so many other things, that kindness and integrity come with the soul.

author's note

The descriptions in *The Sociopath Next Door* do not identify individuals. At the very heart of psychotherapy is the precept of confidentiality, and as usual I have taken the most exacting measures to preserve the privacy of all real persons. All names are fictitious, and all other recognizable features have been changed. Some individuals who appear in the book willingly gave their consent to be anonymously portrayed. In these cases, no information has been included that might in any way identify them.

The story in the chapter entitled "Groundhog Day" is fiction. Otherwise, the people, events, and conversations presented here are taken from my twenty-five-year practice of psychology. However, because of my commitment to confidentiality, the people and circumstances portrayed in these pages are composite in nature; that is to say, each case represents a great many individuals whose characteristics and experiences have been adopted conceptually, carefully altered in their specifics, and combined to form an illustrative character. Any resemblance of such a composite character to any actual person is entirely coincidental.

INTRODUCTION

imagine

Minds differ still more than faces.

—*Voltaire*

Imagine—if you can—not having a conscience, none at all, no feelings of guilt or remorse no matter what you do, no limiting sense of concern for the well-being of strangers, friends, or even family members. Imagine no struggles with shame, not a single one in your whole life, no matter what kind of selfish, lazy, harmful, or immoral action you had taken. And pretend that the concept of responsibility is unknown to you, except as a burden others seem to accept without question, like gullible fools. Now add to this strange fantasy the ability to conceal from other people that your psychological makeup is radically different from theirs. Since everyone simply assumes that conscience is universal among human beings, hiding the fact that you are conscience-free is nearly effortless. You are not held back from any of your desires by guilt or shame, and you are never confronted by others for your cold-bloodedness. The ice water in your veins is so bizarre, so completely outside of their personal experience, that they seldom even guess at your condition.

In other words, you are completely free of internal restraints, and your unhampered liberty to do just as you please, with no pangs of conscience, is conveniently invisible to the world. *You can do anything at all,* and still your strange advantage over the majority of people, who are kept in line by their consciences, will most likely remain undiscovered.

How will you live your life? What will you do with your huge and secret advantage, and with the corresponding handicap of other people (conscience)? The answer will depend largely on just what your desires happen to be, because people are not all the same. Even the profoundly unscrupulous are not all the same. Some people—whether they have a conscience or not—favor the ease of inertia, while others are filled with dreams and wild ambitions. Some human beings are brilliant and talented, some are dull-witted, and most, conscience or not, are somewhere in between. There are violent people and nonviolent ones, individuals who are motivated by blood lust and those who have no such appetites.

Maybe you are someone who craves money and power, and though you have no vestige of conscience, you do have a magnificent IQ. You have the driving nature and the intellectual capacity to pursue tremendous wealth and influence, and you are in no way moved by the nagging voice of conscience that prevents other people from doing everything and anything they have to do to succeed. You choose business, politics, the law, banking, or international development, or any of a broad array of other power professions, and you pursue your career with a cold passion that tolerates none of the usual moral or legal incumbrances. When it is expedient, you doctor the accounting and shred the evidence, you stab your employees and your clients (or your constituency) in the back, marry for money, tell lethal premeditated lies to people who trust you, attempt to ruin colleagues who are powerful or eloquent, and simply steamroll over groups who are dependent and voiceless. And all of this you do with the exquisite freedom that results from having no conscience whatsoever.

You become unimaginably, unassailably, and maybe even globally successful. Why not? With your big brain, and no conscience to rein in your schemes, *you can do anything at all.*

Or no—let us say you are not quite such a person. You are ambitious, yes, and in the name of success you are willing to do all manner of things that people with conscience would never consider, but you are not an intellectually gifted individual. Your intelligence is above average perhaps, and people think of you as smart, maybe even very smart. But you know in your heart of hearts that you do not have the cognitive wherewithal, or the creativity, to reach the careening heights of power you secretly dream about, and this makes you resentful of the world at large, and envious of the people around you.

As this sort of person, you ensconce yourself in a niche, or maybe a series of niches, in which you can have some amount of control over small numbers of people. These situations satisfy a little of your desire for power, although you are chronically aggravated at not having more. It chafes to be so free of the ridiculous inner voice that inhibits others from achieving great power, without having enough talent to pursue the ultimate successes yourself. Sometimes you fall into sulky, rageful moods caused by a frustration that no one but you understands.

But you do enjoy jobs that afford you a certain undersupervised control over a few individuals or small groups, preferably people and groups who are relatively helpless or in some way vulnerable. You are a teacher or a psychotherapist, a divorce lawyer or a high school coach. Or maybe you are a consultant of some kind, a broker or a gallery owner or a human services director. Or maybe you do not have a paid position and are instead the president of your condominium association, or a volunteer hospital worker, or a parent.

Whatever your job, you manipulate and bully the people who are under your thumb, as often and as outrageously as you can without getting fired or held accountable. You do this for its own sake, even when it serves no purpose except to give you a thrill. Making people jump means you have power—or this is the way you see it—and bullying provides you with an adrenaline rush. It is fun.

Maybe you cannot be the CEO of a multinational corporation, but you can frighten a few people, or cause them to scurry around like chickens, or steal from them, or—maybe best of all—create situations that cause them to feel bad about themselves. And this is power, especially when the people you manipulate are superior to you in some way. Most invigorating of all is to bring down people who are smarter or more accomplished than you, or perhaps classier, more attractive or popular or morally admirable. This is not only good fun; it is existential vengeance. And without a conscience, it is amazingly easy to do. You quietly lie to the boss or to the boss's boss, cry some crocodile tears, or sabotage a coworker's project, or gaslight a patient (or a child), bait people with promises, or provide a little misinformation that will never be traced back to you.

Or now let us say you are a person who has a proclivity for violence or for seeing violence done. You can simply murder your coworker, or have her murdered—or your boss, or your ex-spouse, or your wealthy lover's spouse, or anyone else who bothers you. You have to be careful, because if you slip up, you may be caught and punished by the system. But you will never be confronted by your conscience, because you have no conscience. If you decide to kill, the only difficulties will be the external ones. Nothing inside of you will ever protest.

Provided you are not forcibly stopped, *you can do anything at all.* If you are born at the right time, with some access to family fortune, and you have a special talent for whipping up other people's hatred and sense of deprivation, you can arrange to kill large numbers of unsuspecting people. With enough money, you can accomplish this from far away, and you can sit back safely and watch in satisfaction. In fact, terrorism (done from a distance) is the ideal occupation for a person who is possessed of blood lust and no conscience, because if you do it just right, you may be able to make a whole nation jump. And if that is not power, what is?

Or let us imagine the opposite extreme: You have no interest in power. To the contrary, you are the sort of person who really does not want much of anything. Your only real ambition is not to have to exert yourself to get by. You do not want to work like everyone else does. Without a conscience, you can nap or pursue your hobbies or watch television or just hang out somewhere all day long. Living a bit on the fringes, and with some handouts from relatives and friends, you can do this indefinitely. People may whisper to one another that you are an underachiever, or that you are depressed, a sad case, or, in contrast, if they get angry, they may grumble that you are lazy. When they get to know you better, and get really angry, they may scream at you and call you a loser, a bum. But it will never occur to them that you literally do not have a conscience, that in such a fundamental way, your very mind is not the same as theirs.

The panicked feeling of a guilty conscience never squeezes at your heart or wakes you in the middle of the night. Despite your lifestyle, you never feel irresponsible, neglectful, or so much as embarrassed, although for the sake of appearances, sometimes you pretend that you do. For example, if you are a decent observer of people and what they react to, you may adopt a lifeless facial expression, say how ashamed of your life you are, and talk about how rotten you feel. This you do only because it is more convenient to have people think you are depressed than it is to have them shouting at you all the time, or insisting that you get a job.

You notice that people who do have a conscience feel guilty when they harangue someone they believe to be "depressed" or "troubled." As a matter of fact, to your further advantage, they often feel obliged to take care of such a person. If, despite your relative poverty, you can manage to get yourself into a sexual relationship with someone, this person—who does not suspect what you are really like—may feel particularly obligated. And since all you want is not to have to work, your financier does not have to be especially rich, just reliably conscience-bound.

I trust that imagining yourself as any of these people feels insane to you, because such people are insane, dangerously so. Insane but real—they even have a label. Many mental health professionals refer to the condition of little or no conscience as "antisocial personality disorder," a noncorrectable disfigurement of character that is now thought to be present in about 4 percent of the population—that is to say, one in twenty-five people. This condition of missing conscience is called by other names, too, most often "sociopathy," or the somewhat more familiar term, *psychopathy*. Guiltlessness was in fact the first personality disorder to be recognized by psychiatry, and terms that have been used at times over the past century include *manie sans délire, psychopathic inferiority, moral insanity,* and *moral imbecility*.

According to the current bible of psychiatric labels, the *Diagnostic and Statistical Manual of Mental Disorders IV* of the American Psychiatric Association, the clinical diagnosis of "antisocial personality disorder" should be considered when an individual possesses at least three of the following seven characteristics: (1) failure to conform to social norms; (2) deceitfulness, manipulativeness; (3) impulsivity, failure to plan ahead; (4) irritability, aggressiveness; (5) reckless disregard for the safety of self or others; (6) consistent irresponsibility; (7) lack of remorse after having hurt, mistreated, or stolen from another person. The presence in an individual of any three of these "symptoms," taken together, is enough to make many psychiatrists suspect the disorder.

Other researchers and clinicians, many of whom think the APA's definition describes simple "criminality" better than true "psychopathy" or "sociopathy," point to additional documented characteristics of sociopaths as a group. One of the more frequently observed of these traits is a glib and superficial charm that allows the true sociopath to seduce other people, figuratively or literally—a kind of glow or charisma that, initially, can make the sociopath seem more charming or more interesting than most of the normal people around him. He or she is more spontaneous, or more intense, or somehow more "complex," or sexier, or more entertaining than everyone else. Sometimes this "sociopathic charisma" is accompanied by a grandiose sense of self-worth that may be compelling at first, but upon closer inspection may seem odd or perhaps laughable. ("Someday the world will realize how special I am," or "You know that after me, no other lover will do.")

In addition, sociopaths have a greater than normal need for stimulation, which results in their taking frequent social, physical, financial, or legal risks. Characteristically, they can charm others into attempting dangerous ventures with them, and as a group they are known for their pathological lying and conning, and their parasitic relationships with "friends." Regardless of how educated or highly placed as adults, they may have a history of early behavior problems, sometimes including drug use or recorded juvenile delinquency, and always including a failure to acknowledge responsibility for any problems that occurred.

And sociopaths are noted especially for their shallowness of emotion, the hollow and transient nature of any affectionate feelings they may claim to have, a certain breathtaking callousness. They have no trace of empathy and no genuine interest in bonding emotionally with a mate. Once the surface charm is scraped off, their marriages are loveless, one-sided, and almost always short-term. If a marriage partner has any value to the sociopath, it is because the partner is viewed as a possession, one that the sociopath may feel *angry* to lose, but never sad or accountable.

All of these characteristics, along with the "symptoms" listed by the American Psychiatric Association, are the behavioral manifestations of what is for most of us an unfathomable psychological condition, the absence of our essential seventh sense—conscience.

Crazy, and frightening—and real, in about 4 percent of the population.

But what does 4 percent really mean to society? As points of reference to problems we hear about more often, consider the following statistics: The prevalence rate for anorexic eating disorders is estimated at 3.43 percent, deemed to be nearly epidemic, and yet this figure is a fraction lower than the rate for antisocial personality. The high-profile disorders classed as schizophrenia occur in only about 1 percent of us—a mere quarter of the rate of antisocial personality—and the Centers for Disease Control and Prevention say that the rate of colon cancer in the United States, considered "alarmingly high," is about 40 per 100,000—one hundred times lower than the rate of antisocial personality. Put more succinctly, there are more sociopaths among us than people who suffer from the much-publicized disorder of anorexia, four times as many sociopaths as schizophrenics, and one hundred times as many sociopaths as people diagnosed with a known scourge such as colon cancer.

As a therapist, I specialize in the treatment of psychological trauma survivors. Over the last twenty-five years, my practice has included hundreds of adults who have been in psychological pain every day of their lives on account of early childhood abuse or some other horrendous past experience. As I have detailed in case studies in *The Myth of Sanity*, my trauma patients suffer from a host of torments, including chronic anxiety, incapacitating depression, and dissociative mental states, and, feeling that their time on earth was unbearable, many of them have come to me after recovering from attempts to commit suicide. Some have been traumatized by natural and man-made disasters such as earthquakes and wars, but most of them have been controlled and psychologically shattered by individual human perpetrators, often sociopaths—sometimes sociopathic strangers, but more typically sociopathic parents, older relatives, or siblings. In helping my patients and their families cope with the harm done to their lives, and in studying their case histories, I have learned that the damage caused by the sociopaths among us is deep and lasting, often tragically lethal, and startlingly common. Working with hundreds of survivors, I have become convinced that dealing openly and directly with the facts about sociopathy is a matter of urgency for us all.

About one in twenty-five individuals are sociopathic, meaning, essentially, that they do not have a conscience. It is not that this group fails to grasp the difference between good and bad; it is that the distinction fails to limit their behavior. The intellectual difference between right and wrong does not bring on the emotional sirens and flashing blue lights, or the fear of God, that it does for the rest of us. Without the slightest blip of guilt or remorse, *one in twenty-five people can do anything at all.*

The high incidence of sociopathy in human society has a profound effect on the rest of us who must live on this planet, too, even those of us who have not been clinically traumatized. The individuals who constitute this 4 percent drain our relationships, our bank accounts, our accomplishments, our self-esteem, our very peace on earth. Yet surprisingly, many people know nothing about this disorder, or if they do, they think only in terms of violent psychopathy—murderers, serial killers, mass murderers—people who have conspicuously broken the law many times over, and who, if caught, will be imprisoned, maybe even put to death by our legal system. We are not commonly aware of, nor do we usually identify, the larger number of nonviolent sociopaths among us, people who often are not blatant lawbreakers, and against whom our formal legal system provides little defense.

Most of us would not imagine any correspondence between conceiving an ethnic genocide and, say, guiltlessly lying to one's boss about a coworker. But the psychological correspondence is not only there; it is chilling. Simple and profound, the link is the absence of the inner mechanism that beats up on us, emotionally speaking, when we make a choice we view as immoral, unethical, neglectful, or selfish. Most of us feel mildly guilty if we eat the last piece of cake in the kitchen, let alone what we would feel if we intentionally and methodically set about to hurt another person. Those who have no conscience at all are a group unto themselves, whether they be homicidal tyrants or merely ruthless social snipers.

The presence or absence of conscience is a deep human division, arguably more significant than intelligence, race, or even gender. What differentiates a sociopath who lives off the labors of others from one who occasionally robs convenience stores, or from one who is a contemporary robber baron—or what makes the difference between an ordinary bully and a sociopathic murderer—is nothing more than social status, drive, intellect, blood lust, or simple opportunity. What distinguishes all of these people from the rest of us is an utterly empty hole in the psyche, where there should be the most evolved of all humanizing functions.

For something like 96 percent of us, conscience is so fundamental that we seldom even think about it. For the most part, it acts like a reflex. Unless temptation is extremely great (which, thankfully, on a day-to-day basis it usually is not), we by no means reflect on each and every moral question that comes our way. We do not seriously ask ourselves, Shall I give my child lunch money today, or not? Shall I steal my coworker's briefcase today, or not? Shall I walk out on my spouse today, or not? Conscience makes all of these decisions for us, so quietly, automatically, and continually that, in our most creative flights of imagination, we would not be able to conjure the image of an existence without conscience. And so, naturally, when someone makes a truly conscienceless choice, all we can produce are explanations that come nowhere near the truth: She forgot to give lunch money to her child. That person's coworker must have misplaced her briefcase. That person's spouse must have been impossible to live with. Or we come up with labels that, provided we do not inspect too closely, almost explain another person's antisocial behavior: He is "eccentric," or "artistic," or "really competitive," or "lazy," or "clueless," or "always such a rogue."

Except for the psychopathic monsters we sometimes see on television, whose actions are too horrific to explain away, conscienceless people are nearly always invisible to us. We are keenly interested in how smart we are, and in the intelligence level of other people. The smallest child can tell the difference between a girl and a boy. We fight wars over race. But as to what is possibly the single most meaningful characteristic that divides the human species—the presence or absence of conscience—we remain effectively oblivious.

Very few people, no matter how educated they are in other ways, know the meaning of the word *sociopathic.* Far less do they understand that, in all probability, the word could be properly applied to a handful of people they actually know. And even after we have learned the label for it, being devoid of conscience is impossible for most human beings to fantasize about. In fact, it is difficult to think of another experience that quite so eludes empathy. Total blindness, clinical depression, profound cognitive deficit, winning the lottery, and a thousand other extremes of human experience, even psychosis, are accessible to our imaginations. We have all been lost in the dark. We have all been somewhat depressed. We have all felt stupid, at least once or twice. Most of us have made the mental list of what we would do with a windfall fortune. And in our dreams at night, our thoughts and our images are deranged.

But not to care *at all* about the effects of our actions on society, on friends, on family, on our *children*? What on earth would that be like? What would we do with ourselves? Nothing in our lives, waking or sleeping, informs us. The closest we come, perhaps, is the experience of being in so much physical pain that our ability to reason or act is temporarily paralyzed. But even in pain there is guilt. Absolute guiltlessness defies the imagination.

Conscience is our omniscient taskmaster, setting the rules for our actions and meting out emotional punishments when we break the rules. We never asked for conscience. It is just there, all the time, like skin or lungs or heart. In a manner of speaking, we cannot even take credit. And we cannot imagine what we would feel like without it.

Guiltlessness is uniquely confusing as a medical concept, too. Quite unlike cancer, anorexia, schizophrenia, depression, or even the other "character disorders," such as narcissism, sociopathy would seem to have a moral aspect. Sociopaths are almost invariably seen as bad or diabolical, even by (or perhaps especially by) mental health professionals, and the sentiment that these patients are somehow morally offensive and scary comes across vividly in the literature.

Robert Hare, a professor of psychology at the University of British Columbia, has developed an inventory called the *Psychopathy Checklist,* now accepted as a standard diagnostic instrument for researchers and clinicians worldwide. Of his subjects, Hare, the dispassionate scientist, writes, "Everyone, including the experts, can be taken in, manipulated, conned, and left bewildered by them. A good psychopath can play a concerto on *anyone's* heartstrings. . . . Your best defense is to understand the nature of these human predators." And Hervey Cleckley, author of the 1941 classic text *The Mask of Sanity,* makes this complaint of the psychopath: "Beauty and ugliness, except in a very superficial sense, goodness, evil, love, horror, and humor have no actual meaning, no power to move him."

The argument can easily be made that "sociopathy" and "antisocial personality disorder" and "psychopathy" are misnomers, reflecting an unstable mix of ideas, and that the absence of conscience does not really make sense as a psychiatric category in the first place. In this regard, it is crucial to note that all of the other psychiatric diagnoses (including narcissism) involve some amount of personal distress or misery for the individuals who suffer from them. Sociopathy stands alone as a "disease" that causes no *dis-ease* for the person who has it, no subjective discomfort. Sociopaths are often quite satisfied with themselves and with their lives, and perhaps for this very reason there is no effective "treatment." Typically, sociopaths enter therapy only when they have been court-referred, or when there is some secondary gain to be had from being a patient. Wanting to get better is seldom the true issue. All of this begs the question of whether the absence of conscience is a psychiatric disorder or a legal designation—or something else altogether.

Singular in its ability to unnerve even seasoned professionals, the concept of sociopathy comes perilously close to our notions of the soul, of evil versus good, and this association makes the topic difficult to think about clearly. And the unavoidable them-versus-us nature of the problem raises scientific, moral, and political issues that boggle the mind. How does one scientifically study a phenomenon that appears to be, in part, a moral one? Who should receive our professional help and support, the "patients" or the people who must endure them? Since psychological research is generating ways to "diagnose" sociopathy, whom should we test? Should anyone be tested for such a thing in a free society? And if someone has been clearly identified as a sociopath, what, if anything, can society do with that information? No other diagnosis raises such politically and professionally incorrect questions, and sociopathy, with its known relationship to behaviors ranging from spouse battering and rape to serial murder and warmongering, is in some sense the last and most frightening psychological frontier.

Indeed, the most unnerving questions are seldom even whispered: Can we say for sure that sociopathy does not work for the individual who has it? Is sociopathy a disorder at all, or is it functional? Just as unwelcome is the uncertainty on the flip side of that coin: Does *conscience* work for the individual, or group, who has it? Or is conscience, as more than one sociopath has implied, simply a psychological corral for the masses? Whether we speak them out loud or not, doubts like these implicitly loom large on a planet where for thousands of years, and right up to the present moment, the most universally famous names have always belonged to those who could manage to be amoral on a large-enough scale. And in our present-day culture, using other people has become almost trendy, and unconscionable business practices appear to yield unlimited wealth. On a personal level, most of us have examples from our own lives in which someone unscrupulous has won, and there are times when having integrity begins to feel like merely playing the fool.

Is it the case that cheaters never prosper, or is it true, after all, that nice guys finish last? Will the shameless minority really inherit the earth?

Such questions reflect a central concern of this book, a theme that occurred to me just after the catastrophes of September 11, 2001, propelled all people of conscience into anguish, and some into despair. I am usually an optimistic person, but at that time, along with a number of other psychologists and students of human nature, I feared that my country and many others would fall into hate-filled conflicts and vengeful wars that would preoccupy us for many years to come. From nowhere, a line from a thirty-year-old apocalyptic song invaded my thoughts whenever I tried to relax or sleep: "Satan, laughing, spreads his wings." The winged Satan in my mind's eye, roaring with cynical laughter and rising from the wreckage, was not a terrorist, but a demonic manipulator who used the terrorists' acts to ignite the kindling of hatred all over the globe.

I became interested in my particular topic of sociopathy versus conscience during a phone conversation with a colleague of mine, a good man who is normally upbeat and full of encouragement but who was at that moment stunned and demoralized along with the rest of the world. We were discussing a mutual patient whose suicidal symptoms had become alarmingly worse, apparently on account of the disasters in the United States (and who has improved a great deal since then, I am relieved to report). My colleague was saying how guilty he felt because he was torn apart himself and might not have the usual amount of emotional energy to give to the patient. This extraordinarily caring and responsible therapist, overwhelmed by events, like everyone else, believed he was being remiss. In the middle of judging himself, he stopped, sighed, and said to me in a weary voice highly uncharacteristic of him, "You know, sometimes I wonder, Why *have* a conscience? It just puts you on the losing team."

I was very much taken aback by his question, mostly because cynicism was so unlike this man's usual hale and hearty frame of mind. After a moment, I replied with another question. I said, "So tell me, Bernie. If you had a choice, I mean really, literally had a choice in the matter—which you don't, of course—would you choose to have a conscience like you do, or would you prefer to be sociopathic, and capable of . . . well, anything at all?"

He considered this and said, "You're right" (although I had not meant to imply telepathy). "I'd choose to have a conscience."

"Why?" I pressed him.

There was a pause and then a long, drawn-out "Well . . ." Finally, he said, "You know, Martha, I don't know why. I just know I'd choose conscience."

And maybe I was thinking too wishfully, but it seemed to me that after he made this statement, there was a subtle change in Bernie's voice. He sounded slightly less defeated, and we started to talk about what one of our professional organizations planned to do for the people in New York and Washington.

After that conversation, and for a very long time, I remained intrigued by my colleague's question, "Why have a conscience?" and by his preference to be conscience-bound rather than conscience-free, and by the fact that he did not know why he would make this choice. A moralist or a theologian might well have answered, "Because it's right," or "Because I want to be a good person." But my friend the psychologist could not give a *psychological* answer.

I feel strongly that we need to know the psychological reason. Especially now, in a world that seems ready to self-destruct with global business scams, terrorism, and wars of hatred, we need to hear why, *in a psychological sense,* being a person of conscience is preferable to being a person unfettered by guilt or remorse. In part, this book is my answer, as a psychologist, to that question, "Why have a conscience?" To get to the reasons, I first discuss people who are without conscience, the sociopaths—how they behave, how they feel—so that we can look more meaningfully into the value, for the other 96 percent of us, of possessing a trait that can be aggravating, painful, and—yes, it is true—limiting. What follows is a psychologist's celebration of the still small voice, and of the great majority of human beings who find themselves graced with a conscience. It is a book for those of us who cannot imagine any other way to live.

The book is also my attempt to warn good people about "the sociopath next door," and to help them cope. As a psychologist and as a person, I have seen far too many lives nearly obliterated by the choices and acts of a conscienceless few. These few are both dangerous and remarkably difficult to identify. Even when they are not physically violent—and especially when they are familiar and close to us—they are all too capable of mangling individual lives, and of making human society as a whole an unsafe place to be. To my mind, this dominance over the rest of us by people who have no conscience at all constitutes an especially widespread and appalling example of what novelist F. Scott Fitzgerald referred to as "the tyranny of the weak." And I believe that all people of conscience should learn what the everyday behavior of these people looks like, so they can recognize and deal effectively with the morally weak and the ruthless.

Where conscience is concerned, we seem to be a species of extremes. We have only to turn on our televisions to see this bewildering dichotomy, to encounter images of people on their hands and knees rescuing a puppy from a drainage pipe, followed by reports of other human beings slaughtering women and children and stacking the corpses. And in our ordinary daily lives, though perhaps not so dramatically, we see the contrasts just as plentifully. In the morning, someone cheerfully goes out of her way to hand us the ten-dollar bill that we dropped, and in the afternoon, another person, grinning, goes out of his way to cut us off in traffic.

Given the radically contradictory behavior we witness every day, we must talk openly about both extremes of human personality and behavior. To create a better world, we need to understand the nature of people who routinely act against the common good, and who do so with emotional impunity. Only by seeking to discover the nature of ruthlessness can we find the many ways people can triumph over it, and only by recognizing the dark can we make a genuine affirmation of the light.

It is my hope that this book will play some part in limiting the sociopath's destructive impact on our lives. As individuals, people of conscience can learn to recognize "the sociopath next door," and with that knowledge work to defeat his entirely self-interested aims. At the very least, they can protect themselves and their loved ones from his shameless maneuverings.

ONE

the seventh sense

Virtue is not the absence of vices or the avoidance of moral dangers; virtue is a vivid and separate thing, like pain or a particular smell.

—*G. K. Chesterton*

This morning, Joe, a thirty-year-old attorney, is running five minutes late for an extremely important meeting that, with or without him, will start promptly at eight o'clock. He needs to keep up a good impression with the more senior members of his firm, which means just about everybody, and he would like to have the first word with these wealthy clients, whose concerns include Joe's budding specialty of estate planning. He has been preparing his agenda for days because he feels there is a lot at stake, and he very much wants to be in the conference room at the start of the meeting.

Unfortunately, the furnace in Joe's town house suddenly stopped making heat in the middle of the night. Freezing and pacing, afraid the pipes would burst, he had to wait for the emergency repairman from the fuel company before he could leave for work this morning. When the man showed up, Joe let him in and then, desperate to get to the meeting, abandoned him in the town house to fix the furnace, hoping the fellow would prove reasonably honest. At last, Joe was able to race to his Audi and set off for the office, but with only twenty-five minutes left to make a thirty-minute drive. He resolved to bend the rules a little and make up the time.

Now Joe is speeding along a familiar route to work, clenching his teeth and swearing under his breath at the slow drivers, at all the drivers really. He reinterprets a couple of red lights, passes a line of traffic by using the breakdown lane, and clings frantically to the hope that he can somehow make it to the office by 8:00. When he hits three green lights in a row, he thinks that he may just succeed. With his right hand, he reaches over to touch the overnight bag in the passenger's seat, to reassure himself that he remembered to bring it. In addition to everything else, he has to catch a 10:15 plane to New York this morning, a trip for the firm, and there will certainly not be time after the meeting to go back home for his things. His hand contacts the cushiony leather of the bag—it is there and packed.

And at this very moment, Joe remembers. He forgot to feed Reebok. Reebok is Joe's three-year-old blond Labrador retriever, so named because, before he got too busy at the firm, Joe used to take early-morning runs with his enthusiastic new pet. When work took over and the morning routine changed, Joe fenced in the small backyard and installed a doggy door in the basement, allowing the dog solo access to the outside. At this point, runs together in the park are weekends only. But exercise or not, Reebok consumes several pounds of Science Diet every week, along with a huge assortment of leftover human food and at least one full box of jumbo bone treats. The young dog's appetite is stupendous, and he seems to live quite happily for two pleasures alone—his time with Joe, and his food.

Joe got Reebok as a puppy, because when Joe was a boy, his father would not let him have a pet, and he had vowed to himself that when he was grown up and successful, he would have a dog, a big one. At first, Reebok had been not very different from the Audi, another acquisition, a marker of Joe's independence and material prosperity. But soon Joe had fallen in love with the animal himself. How could he not? Reebok adored Joe unconditionally, and from puppyhood had followed him around the house as if Joe were the center of all that was good in the universe. As his puppy grew to doghood, Joe realized that this creature had as distinct and individual a personality as any human being, and that his liquid brown eyes contained at least as much soul. Now, whenever Joe looks into those eyes, Reebok wrinkles his soft beige brow into several folded-carpet furrows and stares back. In this way, the sweet, ungainly dog appears preternaturally thoughtful, as if he can read Joe's mind and is concerned.

Sometimes when there is a business trip, like today, Joe is gone from home for a day and a half, or even a little longer, and each time he comes back, Reebok greets him at the door with bounding joy and instantaneous forgiveness. Before he takes one of these trips, Joe always leaves large mixing bowls full of food and water for Reebok to consume in his absence, which Reebok does easily. But this time, between the furnace problem and his panic about the 8:00 meeting, Joe forgot. The dog has no food and maybe even no water, and no way to get any until tomorrow evening, when Joe returns from his trip.

Maybe I can call someone to help out, Joe thinks desperately. But no. He is between girlfriends at present, and so no one has a key to his house.

The impossibility of his situation begins to dawn on him, and he grips the steering wheel even harder. He absolutely must make this meeting, and he can be there on time if he just keeps going. But what about Reebok? He will not starve to death in a day and a half, Joe knows, but he will be miserable—and the water—how long does it take an animal to die of dehydration? Joe has no idea. Still driving as fast as the traffic will bear, he tries to think about his options. The available choices tumble over one another in a rush. He can attend the 8:00 meeting and then go home and feed the dog, but that will make him miss his 10:15 flight, and the trip is even more important than the meeting. He can go to the meeting and leave in the middle.

No, that would be seen as offensive. He can try to get a later flight, but then he will be very late for his appointment in New York, may even miss it entirely, which could cost him his job. He can ignore the dog until tomorrow. He can turn around now, miss the 8:00 meeting at the firm, take care of the dog, and still make it to the airport for his 10:15 flight.

Like a man in pain, Joe moans loudly and slumps in his seat. Just a few blocks from work, he pulls the car into a spot marked CONSTRUCTION ONLY, dials the office on his cell phone, and tells a secretary to inform those at the morning meeting that he will not be attending. He turns the car around and goes home to feed Reebok.

What Is Conscience?

Amazingly, from a certain point of view, the human being we are calling Joe decides to be absent from an important meeting with some wealthy clients, an event he has spent several days planning for, and where his personal interests quite clearly reside. At first, he does everything he can to get to the meeting on time, risking all the possessions in his town house to a repairman he has never met before, and his own physical safety in his car. And then, at the very last minute, he turns around and goes home to feed a dog, a guileless, wordless creature who could not even so much as reprove Joe for ignoring him. Joe sacrifices a high-stakes desire of his own in favor of an action that no one will witness (except maybe the repairman), a choice that will not enrich him by even one penny. What could possibly cause a young, ambitious lawyer to do such a thing?

Most readers will smile a little when Joe turns his car around. We feel pleased with him for going back to feed his dog. But why are we pleased? Is Joe acting out of *conscience*? Is this what we mean when we make an approving remark about someone's behavior, such as "His *conscience* stopped him"?

What is this invisible, inescapable, frustratingly incorruptible part of us we call "conscience," anyway?

The question is a complicated one, even as it pertains to the simple vignette about Joe and Reebok, because, surprisingly, there are a number of motivations other than conscience that, separately or together, might cause Joe—might cause any of us—to make an apparently self-sacrificing choice. For example, perhaps Joe simply cannot stomach the thought of returning from his New York trip to find a Labrador retriever dehydrated and dead on his kitchen floor. Not knowing how long a dog can survive without water, he is unwilling to take the risk, but his aversion to the horrifying scenario is not exactly conscience. It is something more like revulsion or fear.

Or maybe Joe is motivated by what the neighbors will think if they hear Reebok howling in hunger, or, worse, if they learn the dog has died, alone and trapped, while Joe was on a business trip. How will he ever explain himself to his friends and acquaintances? This worry is not really Joe's conscience, either, but rather his anticipation of serious embarrassment and social rejection. If this is why Joe goes back home to feed his dog, he is hardly the first human being to make a decision based on the dread of what others will think of him, rather than on what he might do if he were sure his actions would remain a complete secret. The opinions of other people keep us all in line, arguably better than anything else.

Or maybe this is all a matter of the way Joe sees himself. Perhaps Joe does not want to view himself, in his own mind's eye, as the kind of wretch who would commit animal abuse, and his self-image as a decent person is crucial enough to him that, when he has no other alternative, he will forgo an important meeting in the service of preserving that image. This is an especially plausible explanation for Joe's behavior. The preservation of self-image is a motivator of some notoriety. In literature and often in historical accounts of human action, dedication to one's own self-regard is referred to as "honor." Lives have been forfeited, wars have been fought over "honor." It is an ancient concern. And in the modern field of psychology, how we view ourselves translates to the newer concept of "self-esteem," a subject about which more psychology books have been written than perhaps any other single topic.

Maybe Joe is willing to relinquish a few career points today in order to feel okay when he looks at himself in the mirror tomorrow, in order to remain "honorable" in his own eyes. This would be laudable and very human—but it is not conscience.

The intriguing truth of the matter is that much of what we do that looks like conscience is motivated by some other thing altogether—fear, social pressure, pride, even simple habit. And where Joe is concerned, a number of readers will strongly favor an explanation other than conscience because some of his behaviors are already questionable. He routinely leaves his young dog alone for many hours at a time, sometimes for nearly two days. This very morning, though he is skipping his meeting and going home to feed the dog, he still intends to make that 10:15 flight and be gone until the following evening. Reebok will have no one to be with, and nowhere to go except a small fenced-in backyard. Consigning a dog to such a situation is not very nice—it reflects, at best, a certain lack of empathy on Joe's part for the animal's social needs.

Still, truth to tell, being nice would not necessarily be conscience, either. For brief periods, any reasonably clever sociopath can act with saintlike niceness for his own manipulative purposes. And people who do possess conscience are often unkind despite themselves, out of ignorance or, as in Joe's case perhaps, inadequate empathy, or just run-of-the-mill psychological denial.

Nice behavior, prudent action, thoughts about how other people will react to us, honorable conduct in the interest of our self-regard—like conscience, all of these have a positive effect on the world at least most of the time, and any or all of them might get the dog fed sometimes, but none can be defined as the individual's conscience. This is because conscience is not a behavior at all, not something that we do or even something that we think or mull over. Conscience is something that we *feel.* In other words, conscience is neither behavioral nor cognitive. Conscience exists primarily in the realm of "affect," better known as *emotion.*

To clarify this distinction, let us take another look at Joe. He is not always nice to his dog, but does he have a conscience? What evidence would cause, say, a psychologist to decide that, when Joe passed up his meeting and went home to rescue Reebok, he was acting out of conscience rather than because of what other people would think, or to preserve his own self-image, or maybe from the noteworthy financial consideration that, three years before, he had paid twelve hundred dollars for a purebred Labrador puppy guaranteed against hip dysplasia and heart disease?

As a psychologist, I am persuaded most by a feature of the story we have not even addressed until now—the fact that Joe feels affection for Reebok. He is *emotionally attached* to his dog. Reebok follows Joe around the house, and Joe likes it. Joe gazes into Reebok's eyes. Reebok has changed Joe from a trophy pet owner to a smitten pet owner. And on account of this attachment, I believe that when Joe gave up his morning plan and went home to take care of his dog, he may possibly have been acting out of conscience. If we could give Joe a truth serum and ask him what was going on inside him at the moment he decided to turn the car around, and he were to say something like, "I just couldn't stand it that Reebok was going to be there hungry and thirsty all that time," then I would be reasonably convinced that Joe was conscience-driven in this situation.

I would be basing my evaluation of Joe on the psychology of conscience itself. Psychologically speaking, conscience is a sense of obligation ultimately based in an emotional attachment to another living creature (often but not always a human being), or to a group of human beings, or even in some cases to humanity as a whole. Conscience does not exist without an emotional bond to someone or something, and in this way conscience is closely allied with the spectrum of emotions we call "love." This alliance is what gives true conscience its resilience and its astonishing authority over those who have it, and probably also its confusing and frustrating quality.

Conscience can motivate us to make seemingly irrational and even self-destructive decisions, from the trivial to the heroic, from missing an 8:00 meeting to remaining silent under torture for the love of one's country. It can drive us in this way only because its fuel is none other than our strongest affections. And witnessing or hearing about an act of conscience, even one as ordinary as feeding a dog, pleases us, because any conscience-bound choice reminds us of the sweet ties that bind. A story about conscience is a story about the connectedness of living things, and in unconscious recognition, we smile at the true nature of the tale. We understand how excruciating Joe's feelings are as he struggles with his conscience, and we smile at Joe and Reebok—because we always smile at lovers.

The History of Conscience

Not everyone has a conscience, this intervening sense of obligation based in our emotional attachments to others. Some people will never experience the exquisite angst that results from letting others down, or hurting them, or depriving them, or even killing them. If the first five senses are the physical ones—sight, hearing, touch, smell, taste—and the "sixth sense" is how we refer to our intuition, then conscience can be numbered seventh at best. It developed later in the evolution of our species and is still far from universal.

To make matters murkier, in the day-to-day course of our lives, we are usually unable to tell the difference between those who possess conscience and those who do not. Could an ambitious young lawyer conceivably have a seventh sense? Yes, conceivably. Could a mother of several young children have a seventh sense? Of course she could. Could a priest, charged with the spiritual welfare of an entire community, be conscience-bound? Let us hope so. Could the powerful political leader of a whole nation of people have a conscience? Certainly.

Or, contrastingly, could any of these people be utterly without conscience? The answer is once again, unnervingly, yes.

The anonymity of "evil" and its maddening refusal to attach itself reliably to any particular societal role, racial group, or physical type has always plagued theologians and, more recently, scientists. Throughout human history, we have tried mightily to pin down "good" and "evil," and to find some way to account for those in our midst who would seem to be inhabited by the latter. In the fourth century, the Christian scholar Saint Jerome introduced the Greek word *synderesis* to describe the innate God-given ability to sense the difference between good and evil. He interpreted Ezekiel's biblical vision of four living creatures emerging from a cloud "with brightness round about it, and fire flashing forth continually." Each creature had the body of a man, but each had four different faces. The face in front was human, the face on the right was that of a lion, the left face was that of an ox, and the face in back was an eagle's. In Jerome's interpretation of Ezekiel's dream, the human face represented the rational part of man, the lion reflected the emotions, the ox symbolized the appetites, and the lofty eagle was "that spark of conscience which was not quenched even in the heart of Cain . . . that makes us, too, feel our sinfulness when we are overcome by evil Desire or unbridled Spirit. . . . And yet in some men we see this conscience overthrown and displaced; they have no sense of guilt or shame for their sins."

Jerome's illustrious contemporary, Augustine of Hippo, agreed with Jerome concerning the nature of conscience. Augustine assured his followers that "men see the moral rules written in the book of light which is called Truth from which all laws are copied."

But a conspicuous problem remained. Since the Truth—the absolute knowledge of good and evil—is given by God to all human beings, why are all human beings not good? Why do we "see this conscience overthrown and displaced" in some people? And this question remained at the center of the theological discussion about conscience for many centuries. Despite the sticky wicket, the alternative suggestion—the proposal that only some people had conscience—was impossible to make, because it would have meant that by withholding the Truth from a few of His servants, God Himself had created evil in the world and had distributed it, in seeming randomness, among all the types and enterprises of humanity.

A solution to the theological dilemma over conscience seemed to come in the thirteenth century, when Thomas Aquinas proposed a roundabout distinction between *synderesis,* Saint Jerome's infallible God-given knowledge of right and wrong, and *conscientia,* which was comprised of mistake-prone human reason as it struggled to reach decisions about behavior. To make its choices concerning which actions to take, Reason was supplied with perfect information from God, but Reason itself was rather weak. In this system, fallible human decision making, not a lack of conscience, is to blame for wrong decisions and actions. Doing wrong is simply making a mistake. In contrast, according to Aquinas, "Synderesis cannot err; it provides principles which do not vary, just as the laws that govern the physical universe do not vary."

To apply this view to our contemporary example—when Joe remembers that his dog is without food and water, God-given innate *synderesis* (conscience) immediately informs him that the absolute right action is to return home and take care of the dog. *Conscientia,* a mental debate about how to behave, then takes this Truth into consideration. The fact that Joe does not turn the car around instantaneously but, instead, spends a few minutes deliberating is the result of the natural weakness of human reason. That Joe does make the right decision in the end means, in Aquinas's scheme, that Joe's moral virtues are, through strengthened Reason, developing in the right direction. Had Joe decided to let the dog go hungry and thirsty, his thereby weakened Reason would have been directing his moral virtues to Hell, theologically speaking.

Getting down to theology's brass tacks, according to the early church fathers, (1) the rules of morality are absolute; (2) all people innately know the absolute Truth; and (3) bad behavior is the result of faulty thinking, rather than a lack of *synderesis,* or conscience, and since we all have a conscience, if only human *reason* were perfect, there would be no bad behavior. And indeed, these are the three beliefs about conscience that have been held by much of the world throughout most of modern history. Their influence on the way we think about ourselves and other people, even today, is inestimable. The third belief is especially hard to let go of. Nearly a millennium after Aquinas made his pronouncement about *synderesis,* when someone consistently behaves in ways we find unconscionable, we call on an updated version of the "weak Reason" paradigm. We speculate that the offender has been deprived, or that his mind is disturbed, or that his early background makes him do it. We remain extremely reluctant to propose the more straightforward explanation that either God or nature simply failed to provide him with a conscience.

For several hundred years, discussions about conscience tended to center around the relationship between human reason and divinely given moral knowledge. A few corollary debates were added, most recently the one over *proportionalism,* a divine loophole wherein Reason asks us to do something "bad" in order to bring about something else that is "good"—a "just war," for example.

But at the beginning of the twentieth century, conscience itself underwent a fundamental transformation, due to the growing acceptance in Europe and the United States of the theories of physician/scientist (and atheist) Sigmund Freud. Freud proposed that in the normal course of development, young children's minds acquired an internalized authority figure, called a *superego,* that would in time replace the actual external authority—the actual external authority being not God but one's own human parents. With his "discovery" of the superego, Freud effectively wrested conscience out of the hands of God and placed it in the anxious clutches of the all-too-human family. This change of address for conscience required some daunting shifts in our centuries-old worldview. Suddenly, our moral guides had feet of clay, and absolute Truth began to submit to the uncertainties of cultural relativism.

Freud's new structural model of the mind did not involve a human part, a lion part, an ox part, and an eagle. Tripartite instead, his vision was of the superego, the ego, and the id. The id was composed of all the sexual and unthinking aggressive instincts we are born with, along with the biological appetites. As such, the id was often in conflict with the demands of a civilized society. In contrast, the ego was the rational, aware part of the mind. It could think logically, make plans, and remember, and because the ego was equipped in these ways, it could interact directly with society and, to varying degrees, get things done for the more primitive id. The superego grew out of the ego as the child incorporated the external rules of his or her parents and of society. The superego eventually became a freestanding force in the developing mind, unilaterally judging and directing the child's behaviors and thoughts. It was the commanding, guilt-brandishing inner voice that said no, even when nobody was around.

The basic concept of superego makes common sense to us. We often observe children internalizing and even enforcing their parents' rules. (Mother frowns and says to her four-year-old daughter, "No shouting in the car." A few minutes later, the same four-year-old points imperiously at her noisy two-year-old sister and shouts, "No shouting in the car!") And most of us, as adults, have heard our own superego. Some of us hear it quite often, in fact. It is the voice in our heads that says to us, Idiot! Why'd you do that? or You know, if you don't finish this report tonight, you'll be sorry, or You'd better get your cholesterol checked. And in the story of Joe and Reebok, Joe's decision to miss his meeting could easily have been made by his superego. For purposes of illustration, let us speculate that Joe's pet-withholding father used to say to him when he was four, "No, little Joey, we can't get a dog. A dog is a tremendous responsibility. When you have a dog, you always have to interrupt what you're doing and take care of it." Joe's adult decision to turn his car around could well have been directed by his superego, which insisted that he fulfill this very dictum.

In a more abstruse manner, Freud himself might have wondered whether Joe's superego had caused Joe to set up his whole morning, unconsciously of course—being in too much of a hurry, forgetting to put out the dog food—such that his father's rule could be "proved," and Joe "punished" for getting a pet. For in Freudian theory, the superego is not just a voice; it is an operator, a subtle and complex manipulator, a prover of points. It prosecutes, judges, and carries out sentences, and it does all this quite outside of our conscious awareness. While the superego, in the best case, can help the individual get along in society, it can also become the most overbearing and perhaps the most destructive part of his personality. According to psychoanalysts, an especially harsh superego, hammering away inside someone's head, can create a lifelong depression, or even propel its poor victim into suicide.

And so Freud introduced the world to the decidedly secular notion that conscience might need to be repaired in some people, and that through psychoanalysis, one might actually repair it.

In addition—more shocking still—Freud and his followers linked the final establishment of the superego to the child's resolution of the Oedipus complex. The Oedipus complex, sometimes called the Electra complex in girls, is formed when the young child begins to realize, between the ages of three and five, that he or she will never completely possess the parent of the opposite sex. In prosaic terms, boys must accept that they will not marry their mothers, and girls must accept that they will not marry their fathers. Oedipal struggles, and the resulting feelings of competition, fear, and resentment toward the parent of the same sex, are so powerful and dangerous to the child's family relationships, according to Freud, that they must be thoroughly "repressed" or kept from awareness, and this "repression" is made possible by a drastic strengthening of the young superego. From this point on, should any sexual feelings arise toward the parent of the opposite sex, or any rivalrous feelings toward the parent of the same sex, these feelings will be vanquished by the dreaded, ruthless weapon of the newly fortified superego—immediate, unbearable guilt. In this way, the superego gains its autonomy and its crowning advantage inside the mind of the child. It is a severe taskmaster installed to serve our need to remain a part of the group.

Whatever else one may think of such theorizing, credit must be given to Freud for understanding that our moral sense was not a one-size-fits-all hermetic code, but was instead dynamic, and intricately tied up with essential family and societal bonds. With his writings on the superego, Freud imparted to an awakening scientific world that our usual respect for law and order was not simply imposed on us from the outside. We obey the rules, we honor the virtues, primarily from an internal need that begins in infancy and early childhood to preserve and remain embraced by our families and the larger human society in which we live.

Conscience Versus Superego

Whether or not one believes that superego is an intrapsychic schemer, or that it is, to use Freud's words, "the heir to the Oedipus complex," superego itself must be acknowledged as a rich and useful concept. As an inner voice acquired through our significant childhood relationships, commenting on our shortcomings and railing against our transgressions, superego is a feature of subjective experience that most people recognize easily. "Don't do that." "You shouldn't feel that way." "Be careful; you'll hurt yourself." "Be nice to your sister." "Clean up that mess you made." "You can't afford to buy that." "Well, that wasn't very smart, was it?" "You've just got to deal with it." "Stop wasting time." Superego yammers at us inside our minds every day of our lives. And some people's superegos are rather more insulting than others.

Still, superego is not the same thing as conscience. It may feel like conscience subjectively, and may be one small part of what conscience is, but superego by itself is not conscience. This is because Freud, as he conceptualized the superego, threw out the baby with the bathwater, in a manner of speaking. In ejecting moral absolutism from psychological thought, he counted out something else too. Quite simply, Freud counted out love, and all of the emotions related to love. Though he often stated that children love their parents in addition to fearing them, the superego he wrote about was entirely fear-based. In his view, just as we fear our parents' stern criticisms when we are children, so do we fear the excoriating voice of superego later on. And fear is all. There is no place in the Freudian superego for the conscience-building effects of love, compassion, tenderness, or any of the more positive feelings.

And conscience, as we have seen in Joe and Reebok, is an intervening sense of obligation based in our emotional attachments to others—all aspects of our emotional attachments—including most especially love, compassion, and tenderness. In fact, the seventh sense, in those individuals who possess it, is primarily love- and compassion-based. We have progressed, over the centuries, from faith in a God-directed *synderesis,* to a belief in a punitive parental superego, to an understanding that conscience is deeply and affectingly anchored in our ability to care about one another. This second progression—from a judge in the head to a mandate of the heart—

involves less cynicism about human nature, more hope for us as a group, and also more personal responsibility and, at times, more personal pain.

As an illustration, imagine that under some impossibly bizarre set of circumstances, one night you take temporary leave of your senses, sneak over to the house of an especially likable neighbor, and, for no particular reason, murder her cat. Just before daybreak, you recover your senses and realize what you have done. What do you feel? What is the specific nature of your guilty reaction? Unseen behind your living room curtain, you watch your neighbor come out to her front step and discover the cat. She falls to her knees. She scoops up her lifeless pet in her arms. She weeps for a very long time.

What is the first thing that happens to you? Does a voice inside your head scream, Thou shalt not kill! You'll go to jail for this!—thus reminding you of the consequences to yourself? Or, instead, do you feel instantly sick that you have murdered an animal and made your neighbor cry in grief? In those first moments of watching your stricken neighbor, which reaction is more likely to befall you? It is a telling question. The answer will probably determine what course of action you will take, and also whether you are influenced only by the strident voice of your superego, or by a genuine conscience.

The same kind of question applies to our old friend Joe. Does he decide to sacrifice his meeting because of the unconscious fear instilled in him in childhood by his father's opinions about dogs, or does he make the sacrifice because he feels awful when he thinks about Reebok's predicament? What directs his choice? Is it pure superego, or is it fully formed conscience? If it is conscience, then Joe's decision to be absent from a scheduled meeting at work is a minor illustration of the fact that, ironically, conscience does not always follow the rules. It places people (and sometimes animals) above codes of conduct and institutional expectations. Fortified with potent emotions, conscience is a glue that holds us together, and it is stickier than it is just. It cherishes humanistic ideals more than laws, and if push comes to shove, conscience may even go to prison. Superego would never do that.

A strict superego berates us, saying, You're being naughty, or You're inadequate. A strong conscience insists, You must take care of him [or her or it or them], no matter what.

Fear-based superego stays behind its dark curtain, accusing us and wringing its hands. Conscience propels us outward in the direction of other people, toward conscious action both minor and great. Attachment-based conscience causes the teenage mother to buy the little jar of creamed peas instead of her favorite fingernail polish. Conscience protects the privileges of intimacy, makes friends keep their promises, prevents the angered spouse from striking back. It induces the exhausted doctor to pick up the phone for his frightened patient at three in the morning. It blows whistles against institutions when lives are endangered. It takes to the streets to protest a war. Conscience is what makes the human rights worker risk her very life. When it is combined with surpassing moral courage, it is Mother Teresa, Mahatma Gandhi, Nelson Mandela, Aung San Suu Kyi.

In small and large ways, genuine conscience changes the world. Rooted in emotional connectedness, it teaches peace and opposes hatred and saves children. It keeps marriages together and cleans up rivers and feeds dogs and gives gentle replies. It makes individual lives better and increases human dignity overall. It is real and compelling, and it would make us crawl out of our skin if we devastated our neighbor.

The problem, as we are about to see, is that not everybody has it. In fact, 4 percent of all people do not have it. Let us turn now to a discussion of such a person—someone who simply has no conscience—and see what he looks like to us.

TWO

ice people: the sociopaths

Conscience is the window of our spirit, evil is the curtain.

—Doug Horton

When Skip was growing up, his family had a vacation cottage by a small lake in the hills of Virginia, where they went for a part of each summer. They vacationed there from the time Skip was eight years old until he went away to high school in Massachusetts. Skip looked forward to his summers in Virginia. There was not a lot to do there, but the one activity he had invented was so much fun that it made up for the general lack of excitement. In fact, sometimes back at grade school in the winter, escaping into his own thoughts while some stupid teacher went on and on about something, he would get a picture of himself playing his game by the warm Virginia lake, and he would chuckle out loud.

Skip was brilliant and handsome, even as a child. "Brilliant and handsome," his parents and his parents' friends and even his teachers would remark over and over. And so they could not understand why his grades were so mediocre, or why, when the time came, he seemed to have so little interest in going out on dates. What they did not know was that from the age of eleven, Skip had been out with plenty of girls, but not quite in the way his parents and teachers were imagining. There was always someone, usually an older girl, who was willing to succumb to Skip's flattery and his charming smile. Often the girl would sneak him into her room, but sometimes he and a girl would simply find a secluded spot on a playground or under the bleachers at the softball field. As for his grades, he really was extremely smart—he could have made straight *A*-plusses—but getting *C*'s was completely effortless, and so that was what he did. Occasionally, he would even get a *B*, which amused him, since he never studied. The teachers liked him, seemed to be almost as vulnerable to his smiles and his compliments as the girls were, and everyone assumed that young Skipper would end up at a good high school and then a decent college, despite his grades.

His parents had a great deal of money, were "megarich," as the other kids put it. On several occasions when he was about twelve, Skip sat at the antique rolltop desk his parents had bought for his bedroom, trying to calculate how much money he would get when they died. He based his calculations on some financial records he had stolen from his father's study. The records were confusing and incomplete, but even though he could not arrive at an exact figure, Skip could see clearly that someday he would be quite rich.

Still, Skip had a problem. He was bored most of the time. The amusements he pursued, even the girls, even fooling the teachers, even thinking about his money, did not keep him energized for longer than half an hour or so. The family wealth held the most promise as an entertainment, but it was not under his control yet—he was still a child. No, the only real relief from boredom was the fun he could have in Virginia. Vacations were a very good time. That first summer, when he was eight, he had simply stabbed the bullfrogs with a scissors, for want of another method. He had discovered that he could take a net from the fishing shed and capture the frogs easily from the mud banks of the lake. He would hold them down on their backs, stab their bulging stomachs, and then turn them back over to watch their stupid jelly eyes go dead as they bled out. Then he would hurl the corpses as far out into the lake as he could, yelling at the dead frogs as they flew, "Too bad for you, you little fuck-face froggy!"

There were so many frogs in that lake. He could spend hours at a time killing them, and still it looked as if there were hundreds and hundreds of them left for tomorrow. But by the end of that first summer, Skip had decided that he could do better. He was tired of stabbing the frogs. It would be so great to blow them up, to have something that would make the fat little squirmers explode, and toward this end he had a really good plan. He knew plenty of older boys back home, and one in particular he knew took a family trip to South Carolina during spring break every April. Skip had heard that fireworks were for sale and easy to get in South Carolina. With a little bribe from Skip, his friend Tim would buy him some fireworks there and smuggle them home in the bottom of his suitcase. Tim would be scared to do it, but with a pep talk from Skip, and enough money, he would. Next summer, Skip would have not scissors but fireworks!

Finding cash around the house was no problem, and the plan worked like a charm. That April, he came up with two hundred dollars for a fireworks variety pack called "Star-Spangled Banner," which he had seen in a gun magazine, and another one hundred dollars to sweeten the deal for Tim. And when Skip finally got his hands on the package, it was a beautiful thing. He had chosen "Star-Spangled Banner" because it contained the largest number of devices small enough to fit, or almost fit, into the mouth of a bullfrog. There was a supply of tiny Roman candles; and some "Lady Fingers," which were slim little red firecrackers; and a bunch of one-inch shells called "Wizards"; and his favorite, some two-inch shells in a box labeled "Mortal Destruction," which had a skull and crossbones blazoned on the front.

That summer, he shoved the devices, one by one, into the mouths of the captured frogs, ignited them, and threw the frogs high into the air over the lake. Or sometimes he would put the ignited frog down, run off, and watch from a distance as the animal exploded on the ground. The displays were magnificent—blood, goo, lights, sometimes a big noise and those colorful flowerlike shapes. So wonderful were the results that soon he began to crave an audience for his genius. One afternoon, he enticed his six-year-old sister, Claire, down to the lake, let her help him capture one of the frogs, and then before her eyes, made an airborne explosion of it. Claire screamed hysterically and ran as fast as her legs would carry her back to the house.

The family's stately "cottage" sat about half a mile from the lake, beyond a serene stand of hundred-foot hemlocks. This was not so far away that Skip's parents had not heard explosive noises, and they imagined that Skipper must be setting off fireworks by the lake. But they had long since realized that he was not the sort of child who could be controlled, and that they needed to choose their battles very carefully. The fireworks issue was not one they chose to deal with, not even when six-year-old Claire came running in to tell her mother that Skipper was blowing up frogs. Skip's mother turned up the record player in the library as loud as it would go, and Claire tried to hide her cat, Emily.

Super Skip

Skip is sociopathic. He has no conscience—no intervening sense of obligation based in emotional attachments to others—and his later life, which we will get to in a moment, provides an instructive example of what an intelligent adult without a conscience can look like.

Just as it is difficult to imagine how we would feel if we had no conscience at all, so it is very hard to use one's imagination to construct an accurate picture of such a person. Amoral and uncaring, does he end up isolated on the edges of society? Does he constantly threaten and snarl and quite possibly drool, devoid as he is of such a fundamental human characteristic? One might easily imagine that Skip grew up to be a killer. In the end, perhaps he murdered his parents for their money. Maybe he wound up dead himself, or in the bowels of a maximum-security prison. Sounds likely, but nothing of the kind actually happened. Skip is still alive, he has never killed anyone, not directly at least, and—so far—he has not seen the inside of any prison. To the contrary, though he has not yet inherited his parents' money, he has become successful and richer than a king. And if you met him now, encountered him as a stranger in a restaurant or on the street, he would look like any other well-groomed middle-aged fellow in a pricey business suit.

How could this possibly be? Did he have a recovery? Did he get better? No. In truth, he got worse. He became Super Skip.

With passing, if not stellar, grades, his charm, and his family's influence, Skip did indeed get into that good boarding school in Massachusetts, and his family breathed a sigh of relief, both for his acceptance by the school and for his relative absence from their lives. His teachers still found him charismatic, but his mother and sister had learned that he was manipulative and spooky. Claire would sometimes speak of "Skipper's weird eyes," and her mother would give her a defeated look that said, I don't want to talk about it. Most everyone else saw only a handsome young face.

When college came around, Skip was accepted into his father's alma mater (and his grandfather's before that), where he became legendary as a party boy and a ladies' man. Graduating with his customary C average, he entered an MBA program at a less prestigious institution, because he had figured out that the business world was a place where he might master the game easily and amuse himself using his natural skills. His grades got no better, but his lifelong ability to charm people and get them to do what he wanted became more refined.

When he was twenty-six, he joined the Arika Corporation, a company that made blasting, drilling, and loading equipment for metal-ore mines. He had intense blue eyes and a stunning smile at all the right moments, and to his new employers he seemed almost magically talented at motivating sales representatives and influencing contacts. For his part, Skip had discovered that manipulating educated adults was no harder than it had been to convince his young friend Tim to buy fireworks in South Carolina, and of course lying, in increasingly elegant ways, came as easily as breathing. Even better, chronically bored Skip relished the pressures of fast-track risk taking and was more than willing to take the big chances that no one else would. Before his third anniversary at the company, he had gone after the copper in Chile and the gold in South Africa, eventually making Arika into the world's third-largest vendor of both shaft and open-pit mining equipment. Arika's founder, whom Skip privately viewed as a fool, was so enchanted with Skip that he gave him a new Ferrari GTB as a "corporate gift."

When he was thirty, Skip married Juliette, the lovely, soft-spoken twenty-three-year-old daughter of a celebrated billionaire who had made his fortune in oil exploration. Skip made sure that Juliette's father saw him as the brilliant, ambitious son he had never had. Skip saw his billionaire father-in-law as what he was, a ticket to just about everything. And, quite accurately, he saw his new wife, Juliette, as a sweet, repressed gentlewoman who would thoroughly accept her role as wife and social coordinator, and who would pretend not to know that Skip's life remained just as devoid of personal responsibility and full of random sexual encounters as it had ever been. She would be attractive and respectable on his arm, and she would keep her mouth shut.

A week before the wedding, Skip's mother, already feeling closer to Juliette than to Skip, wearily inquired of her son, "This marriage . . . Do you really need to do this to her life?" Skip started to ignore her, as he usually did. But then he was apparently struck by something funny, and he replied to her protest with an ear-to-ear grin. "We both know she'll never know what hit her," he said. Skip's mother looked confused for a moment, and then she shuddered.

Married, socially ensconced, and bringing in close to $80 million a year for Arika, Skip was made president of its international division and a member of the board before his thirty-sixth birthday. By this time, he and Juliette had two little girls, completing his public disguise as a family man. His contributions to the business came with a certain price, but nothing that could not be handled in a cost-efficient manner. Employees sometimes complained that he was "insulting" or "vicious," and Arika was sued when a secretary claimed he had broken her arm while trying to force her to sit in his lap. The case was settled out of court with fifty thousand dollars and a gag order for the secretary. Fifty thousand dollars was nothing to the company, relatively speaking. He was "Super Skip," and his employer understood that he was well worth the upkeep.

Of the incident, Skip later remarked privately, "She's insane. She broke her own arm. She struggled with me, the stupid bitch. Why the hell did she put up such a fight?"

After the secretary, there were additional charges of sexual misconduct, but Skip was so valuable to the organization that each time a problem came up, Arika simply disbursed another check to make sure it went away. The other board members began to refer to him as their "company prima donna." As the years passed, he received grants of more than 1 million shares, making him the second-largest individual shareholder, after Arika's founder. And in 2001, at the age of fifty-one, Skip took over as chief executive.

More recently, some of his problems have become slightly less manageable, but with his usual arrogance, Skip is confident he will land on his feet—perhaps a little too confident. In 2003, he was accused of fraud by the Securities and Exchange Commission. He denied the charge, of course, and at present the decision of the SEC is pending.

Playing the Game

No, Skip was not consigned to the edges of society, he does not drool, and he is not (yet) in prison. In fact, he is rich and, in many circles, respected—or at least feared, which masquerades brilliantly as respect. So what is wrong with this picture? Or perhaps the question should be: What is the *worst* part of this picture, the central flaw in Skip's life that makes him into a tragedy despite his success, and into the maker of tragedies for so many others? It is this: Skip has no emotional attachments to other people, none at all. He is cold as ice.

His mother is there to be ignored, or sometimes baited. His sister is there to be tormented. Other women are sexual plunder and nothing more. He has been waiting since childhood for his father to do only one thing—to die and leave his money to Skip. His employees are there to be manipulated and used, as his friends have always been. His wife and even his children are meant for the eyes of the world. They are camouflage. Skip is intellectually gifted, and he is fabulous at the gamesmanship of business. But by far his most impressive talent is his ability to conceal from nearly everyone the true emptiness of his heart—and to command the passive silence of those few who do know.

Most of us are irrationally influenced by appearance, and Skipper has always looked good. He knows just how to smile. He is charming, and we can readily imagine him showering flattery on the boss who gave him the Ferrari, meanwhile thinking him the fool, and underneath it all being incapable of gratitude toward anyone. He lies artfully and constantly, with absolutely no sense of guilt that might give him away in body language or facial expression. He uses sexuality as manipulation and hides his emotional vacancy behind various respectable roles—corporate superstar, son-in-law, husband, father—which are nearly impenetrable disguises.

And if the charm and the sexuality and the role playing somehow fail, Skip uses fear, a sure winner. His iciness is fundamentally scary. Robert Hare writes, "Many people find it difficult to deal with the intense, emotionless, or 'predatory' stare of the psychopath," and for some of the more sensitive people in his life, Skip's intense blue eyes, the ones his sister sees as "weird," may well be those of the dispassionate hunter gazing at his psychological prey. If so, the result will probably be silence.

For even if you know about him, know what his heart is like, and have caught on to his modus operandi, how will you call him out? Whom can you possibly tell, and what will you say? "He's a liar"? "He's crazy"? "He raped me in his office"? "He's got spooky eyes"? "He used to kill frogs"? But this is a leader of the community, in an Armani suit. This is Juliette's beloved husband, and the father of two. This man is the CEO of the Arika Corporation, for goodness sake! Just what are you accusing him of, and what proof do you have? Who is going to sound crazier—chief executive Skip, or his accuser? And sealing his invulnerability, there are those who need Skip to be around for one reason or another, including people who are wealthy and powerful. Are they going to care what you say?

In his unassailability, and in many other ways, Skip is an exemplary sociopath. He has, in the words of the American Psychiatric Association, "a greater than normal need for stimulation," and so he often takes big risks, and he guiltlessly charms others into taking them, too. He has a history of undocumented childhood "behavior problems," obscured by his parents' social privilege. He is deceitful and manipulative. He can be impulsively aggressive with "a reckless disregard for the safety of others," as he was with the employee whose arm he broke, and with the other women whose stories will never be heard. Perhaps the only classic "symptom" Skip does not exhibit is substance abuse. The closest he ever comes to that is one too many scotches after dinner. Otherwise, the picture is complete. He is not genuinely interested in bonding with anyone, he is consistently irresponsible, and he has no remorse.

And so how does all of this turn in his mind? What makes him tick? What exactly does Skip *want*?

Most of us have other people to motivate us and to populate our desires. People drive our wishes and our dreams. People who live with us, people who are far away, beloved people who have died, aggravating people who will not leave, places made sentimental by whom we knew there, even our pets—these fill our hearts and our thoughts. Even the most introverted among us is defined by her relationships, and preoccupied with reactions to and feelings about, antipathies and affections for, other people. Emotional intrigue, romance, nurturing, rejection, and reunion comprise nearly all of our literature and song. We are overwhelmingly relational creatures, and this is true all the way back to our primate ancestors. Jane Goodall says the chimpanzees she observed in Gombe "have a rich repertoire of behaviours that serve to maintain or restore social harmony. . . . The embracing, kissing, patting and holding of hands that serve as greetings after separation . . . The long, peaceful sessions of relaxed social grooming. The sharing of food. The concern for the sick or wounded." And so without our primordial attachments to others, what would we be?

Evidently, we would be the players of a game, one that resembled a giant chess match, with our fellow human beings as the rooks, the knights, and the pawns. For this is the essence of sociopathic behavior and desire. The only thing Skip really wants—the only thing left—is to win.

Skip does not spend any time searching for someone to love. He cannot love. He does not worry about friends or family members who may be sick or in trouble, because he cannot worry about other people. He cares nothing for others, and so he cannot enjoy telling his parents or his wife about his many successes in the business world. He can have dinner with whomever he pleases, but he cannot share the moment with anyone at all. And when his children were born, he was not scared, but neither was he excited. He can derive no real joy from being with them, or from watching them grow up.

But there is one thing Skip can do, and he does this one thing better than almost anyone else: Skip is brilliant at winning. He can dominate. He can bend others to his will. When he was a boy, the frogs died when he decided they should die, his sister screamed when he wanted her to, and now he has gone on to bigger and better games. In a world where people struggle just to make a living, Skip convinced others to make him rich before he was thirty. He can make fools of his well-educated employers and even his billionaire father-in-law. He can cause these otherwise-sophisticated people to jump, and then laugh at them behind their backs. He influences large financial decisions on an international playing field, can turn most such arrangements to his own advantage, and no one protests. Or if someone does complain, he can cut that person off at the knees with just a well-placed word or two. He can frighten people, assault them, break an arm, ruin a career, and his wealthy colleagues will fall all over themselves making sure he never pays the penalties any ordinary person would pay. He believes he can have any woman he wants, and manipulate any man he comes across, including, most recently, everyone at the Securities and Exchange Commission.

He is Super Skip. Strategies and payoffs are the only thrills he knows, and he has spent his entire life getting better at the game. For Skip, the game is everything, and though he is too shrewd to say so, he thinks the rest of us are naïve and stupid for not playing it his way. And this is exactly what happens to the human mind when emotional attachment and conscience are missing. Life is reduced to a contest, and other human beings seem to be nothing more than game pieces, to be moved about, used as shields, or ejected.

Of course, few individuals equal Skip in the level of his IQ or in his physical appearance. By definition, most people, including sociopaths, are average in intelligence and looks, and the games that average sociopaths play are not in the same elite league as Super Skip's global competitions. Many contemporary psychologists, myself included, recall first learning about psychopathy from an educational movie on the subject, viewed when we were college students in the 1970s. The nebbishy case study in the movie is remembered as "Stamp Man," because he devoted his whole life to the unlikely project of stealing postage stamps from United States post offices. He was not interested in possessing the stamps, or in selling them for cash. His only ambition was to execute a simple break-in at night and then find a spot a little distance from the post office he had just robbed, where he could watch the frenzy of the first employees to enter the building in the morning, followed by the emergency arrival of the police. Skinny, pale, and mouselike, the man interviewed in the movie was anything but scary. His intelligence was average at most, and he could never have played Skip's grand international game, with its masterful strategies and billionaire opponents. But he could play his own game, and psychologically, his simple stamp-stealing game was surprisingly similar to Skip's corporate one.

Unlike Skip's, Stamp Man's plans were inelegant and transparent, and he was always discovered and arrested. He had been to court and then to jail countless times, and this was the way he lived his life—robbing, watching, going to jail, getting out of jail, and robbing again. But he was unconcerned, because the eventual outcome of his scheming was irrelevant to him. From his perspective, all that mattered was playing the game and seeing, at least for an hour or so each time, the irrefutable evidence that he, Stamp Man, could *make people jump*. In Stamp Man's opinion, being able to make people jump meant he was winning, and in this way, no less than phenomenally affluent Skip, he illustrates what a sociopath wants. Controlling others—winning—is more compelling than anything (or anyone) else.

Perhaps the ultimate in dominating another person is to take a life, and the psychopathic murderer or cold-blooded serial killer is the first thing many of us imagine when we think of sociopathic deviance. Short of a sociopathic leader who diverts the course of an entire nation, leading it into genocide or unnecessary war, the psychopathic killer is surely the most terrifying example of a psyche without conscience—the most terrifying example, but not the most common one. Homicidal sociopaths are notorious. We read about them in newspapers, hear about them on television, see them portrayed in films, and we are shaken to our core by the knowledge that in our midst there are sociopathic monsters who can kill without passion or remorse. But contrary to popular belief, most sociopaths are not murderers, at least not in the sense that they kill with their own two hands. We can see this from statistics alone. About one in twenty-five people are sociopathic, but outside of prisons, or gangs and other poverty- and war-torn groups, the incidence of murderers in our population is, thankfully, far less.

When sociopathy and blood lust come together in the same person, the result is a dramatic—even a cinematic—nightmare, a horror figure who seems larger than life. But most sociopaths are not mass murderers or serial killers. They are not Pol Pot or Ted Bundy. Instead, most are only life-size, like the rest of us, and can remain unidentified for long periods of time. Most people without conscience are more like Skip or Stamp Man, or the mother who uses her children as tools, or the therapist who deliberately disempowers vulnerable patients, or the seduce-and-manipulate lover, or the business partner who empties the bank account and vanishes, or the charming "friend" who uses people and insists she has not. The methods sociopaths dream up to control others—the schemes contrived to ensure "wins"—are quite various, and only a few of them have to do with physical violence. After all, violence is conspicuous, and unless performed against the utterly powerless, such as children or animals, it is likely to get the perpetrator caught.

In any case, though they are horrifying when they occur, brutal murders are not the likeliest result of consciencelessness. Rather, the *game* is the thing. The prize to be won can run the gamut from world domination to a free lunch, but it is always the same game—controlling, making others jump, "winning." Evidently, winning in this fashion is all that remains of interpersonal meaning when attachment and conscience are absent. When the value of relationships has been reduced to nearly nothing, dominance is sometimes asserted by murdering people. But more often, it is accomplished by killing frogs, or racking up sexual conquests, or seducing and using friends, or exploiting the copper in Chile, or stealing some postage stamps just to see people scramble.

Do Sociopaths Know They Are Sociopaths?

Do sociopaths understand what they are? Do they have some insight into their nature, or, instead, could they read this book from cover to cover and fail to see themselves reflected? In my work, I am often asked these kinds of questions, especially by people whose lives have been derailed by collisions with sociopaths whom they did not recognize as such until it was too late. I do not know exactly why the issue of insight assumes so much importance, except perhaps for our feeling that if a person gets through life totally without conscience, he or she should at least acknowledge that very fact. We feel that if someone is bad, he should be burdened with the knowledge that he is bad. It seems to us the ultimate in injustice that a person could be evil, by our assessment, and still feel fine about himself.

However, this is exactly what seems to happen. For the most part, people whom we assess as evil tend to see nothing at all wrong with their way of being in the world. Sociopaths are infamous for their refusal to acknowledge responsibility for the decisions they make, or for the outcomes of their decisions. In fact, a refusal to see the results of one's bad behavior as having anything to do with oneself—"consistent irresponsibility" in the language of the American Psychiatric Association—is a cornerstone of the antisocial personality diagnosis. Skip illustrated this aspect of his personality when he explained that the employee whose arm he broke had actually broken her own arm when she did not submit to him readily enough. People without conscience provide endless examples of such stunning "I've done nothing wrong" statements. One of the most famous is a quotation from Chicago's sadistic Prohibition gangster, Al Capone: "I am going to St. Petersburg, Florida, tomorrow. Let the worthy citizens of Chicago get their liquor the best they can. I'm sick of the job—it's a thankless one and full of grief. I've been spending the best years of my life as a public benefactor." Other sociopaths do not bother with such convoluted reasoning, or they are not in commanding-enough positions to have anyone listen to their outrageous logic. Instead, when confronted with a destructive outcome that is clearly their doing, they will say, plain and simple, "I never did that," and will to all appearances believe their own direct lie. This feature of sociopathy makes self-awareness impossible, and in the end, just as the sociopath has no genuine relationships with other people, he has only a very tenuous one with himself.

If anything, people without conscience tend to believe their way of being in the world is superior to ours. They often speak of the naïveté of other people and their ridiculous scruples, or of their curiosity about why so many people are unwilling to manipulate others, even in the service of their most important ambitions. Or they theorize that all people are the same—unscrupulous, like them—but are dishonestly playacting something mythical called "conscience." By this latter proposition, the only straightforward and honest people in the world are they themselves. They are being "real" in a society of phonies.

Still, I believe that somewhere buried safely away from consciousness, there may be a faint internal murmuring that something is missing, something that other people have. I say this because I have heard sociopaths speak of feeling "empty" or even "hollow." And I say this because what sociopaths envy, and may seek to destroy as a part of the game, is usually something in the character structure of a person with conscience, and strong characters are often specially targeted by sociopaths. And most of all, I say this because it is human beings who are targeted, rather than the earth itself, or some aspect of the material world. Sociopaths want to play their games with other people. They are not so much interested in challenges from the inanimate. Even the destruction of the World Trade towers was mainly about the people who were in them, and the people who would see and hear about the catastrophe. This simple but crucial observation implies that, in sociopathy, there remains some innate identification with other human beings, a tie with the species itself. However, this thin inborn connection, which enables envy, is one-dimensional and sterile, especially when contrasted with the vast array of complex and highly charged emotional responses most people have to one another and to their fellow human beings as a group.

If all you had ever felt toward another person were the cold wish to "win," how would you understand the meaning of love, of friendship, of caring? You would not understand. You would simply go on dominating, and denying, and feeling superior. Perhaps you would experience a little emptiness sometimes, a remote sense of dissatisfaction, but that is all. And with the wholesale denial of your true impact on other people, how would you understand who you were? Once again, you would not. Like Super Skip himself, Super Skip's mirror can tell only lies. His glass does not show him the iciness of his soul, and the Skip who spent his childhood summers mutilating bullfrogs by an otherwise-peaceful Virginia lake will eventually go to his grave not understanding that his life could have been full of meaning and warmth.

THREE

when normal conscience sleeps

The price of freedom is eternal vigilance.

—Thomas Jefferson

Conscience is a creator of meaning. As a sense of constraint rooted in our emotional ties to one another, it prevents life from devolving into nothing but a long and essentially boring game of attempted dominance over our fellow human beings, and for every limitation conscience imposes on us, it gives us a moment of connectedness with an *other,* a bridge to someone or something outside of our often meaningless schemes. Considering the ice-cold alternative of being someone like Skip, conscience is devoutly to be wished. So the question arises: In the 96 percent of us who are not sociopathic, does conscience ever change? Does it ever waver or weaken—or die?

The truth is that even a normal person's conscience does not operate on the same level all of the time. One of the simplest reasons for this changeability is the fundamental circumstances of living inside a fallible, need-driven human body. When our bodies are exhausted, sick, or injured, all of our emotional functions, including conscience, can be temporarily compromised.

To illustrate this, as he drives along in his car, let us give attorney Joe, owner of Reebok, a dizzying fever of about 102 degrees. We can see right away that his common sense is faltering, since, sick as he is, he is still trying to get to his meeting at work. But what about his moral sense? As a pitiless virus takes possession of his body, what does Joe do when he remembers that his dog Reebok, whom he loves, has no food? In this version of the story, Joe may barely have enough energy to go through with the plans he has already made, let alone be able to think quickly, prioritize on the spot, and redirect himself, as he does in the nonsick–Joe scenario. Feverish and queasy, now his emotional reaction to Reebok's distress is in direct competition with his own misery. Maybe conscience will still prevail. On the other hand, maybe Joe, weakened by illness, no longer possesses the complete strength of his convictions. Following the course of least resistance, maybe he will just keep driving and try to suffer through his original plans, and Reebok, though not altogether forgotten, will be relegated to an emotional back burner for a while.

This is not really how we want to think about Joe, or about ourselves, but it is interesting, and it is true: Our exalted sense of conscience, the bringer of connection and meaning, can at times be significantly affected by something as totally irrelevant to right versus wrong, as unrelated to our moral sensibilities, as the flu—or a missed night's sleep, or a car crash, or a toothache. Normal conscience never disappears, but when the body is weak, conscience can get very sleepy and unfocused.

An assault to the body is one of two things—the other one being great fear—that elevate continued, wide-awake conscience to an heroic level in our eyes. If a person is acutely ill or seriously injured, or afraid, and yet remains true to his or her emotional attachments, we think of that person as courageous. The classic example is the frontline soldier who, though injured himself, rescues his comrade from enemy fire. That we insist on the concept of courage to describe such acts is our tacit acknowledgment that the voice of conscience is commonly outshouted by substantial pain or fear. And in order to care for Reebok, if Joe were to make an extra drive home even with a fever of 102, we might see his behavior as heroic in a minor way. We would do more than just smile at him sentimentally. We might want to pat him on the back.

Another bodily influence on conscience is, strangely enough, hormones. To relate this impairment of conscience succinctly—according to figures from the National Adoption Information Clearinghouse, 15 to 18 percent of recent births in the United States were "unwanted by the mother" at the time of conception. It is fair to assume that some of these pregnancies resulted from ignorance or genuine accident, but to be sure, hundreds of thousands of brand-new Americans are now living the insecure existence of unwanted children simply because a physical appetite eclipsed their parents' consciences for just a few minutes in each case. When speaking of sexual pressures, we acknowledge how difficult it can be to argue with our biological nature, and we raise instances of sustained conscience to the lofty designation of "virtue." Noteworthy is that, by this definition, we are often more "virtuous" at forty than we were at twenty, and this "virtue" is achieved merely through aging.

There are tragic biological subversions of conscience, as well. These include the various schizophrenic disorders that sometimes cause individuals to act based on psychotic delusions. When the human brain is impaired in this way, "The voices told me to do it" is not a joke but a horrifying reality, and for the haunted soul whose psychosis waxes and wanes over time, there is the possibility of "waking" from insanity to find that he has acted on a delusional idea against his own conscience and will.

Fortunately, the pressures our bodies bring to bear on conscience are fairly circumscribed. Outside of combat, situations in which we must make crucial moral decisions while we are severely injured do not happen to us every day, or even every year, and for most people, sexual enthrallment is similarly infrequent. Out-of-control paranoid schizophrenia is relatively rare. Even taken together, the biological limitations on our moral sense do not account for very much of the incomprehensibly bad behavior we can read about in our newspapers or see on our televisions any hour of any day. Schizophrenics are unlikely to be organized terrorists. Toothaches do not cause hate crimes. Unprotected sex does not start wars.

So what does?

Moral Exclusion

Each year on the Fourth of July, the little seaside New England town where I live lights a three-story celebratory bonfire on the beach. Pallets of dry wood are nailed together and artfully stacked on top of one another in a towerlike shape that dominates our quaint landscape for several days before the Fourth. The tower is constructed just so, with enough planks of wood and enough space for airflow in between that it can be counted on to flame up quickly. It is ignited as darkness falls, with the volunteer fire department standing by, hoses at the ready, just in case. The atmosphere is festive. The band plays patriotic songs. There are hot dogs and Slurpees and a fireworks display. When the bonfire has burned out completely, the children return to the beach, where the firemen obligingly drench them with their hoses.

All of this has been a town tradition for sixty years, but not being a big fan of massive fires, I have attended it only once, in 2002, when I was encouraged by friends. I was amazed by the numbers of people who had somehow pressed themselves into our tiny corner of the Atlantic coastline, some of them from fifty or more miles away, and I jostled with the crowd to find a spot close enough to see the fire, but far enough away not to get my eyebrows singed, or so I thought. I had been warned that once the fire got going, there would be more heat than I could imagine, and it was already a ninety-degree day. As the sun began to set, there were hoots and shouts and calls for the tower to be torched, and when flame was finally put to wood, there was a collective gasp. The fire immediately began to engulf the wooden structure like the unstoppable force it was, from the sand upward to a night sky that suddenly blazed. And then came the heat. With the feel of a near-solid object, a wall of unbearable, even frightening superheated air rolled outward from the fire in waves of increasing intensity, taking the crowd by surprise and pushing us away en masse. Each time I thought I was far enough away, I had to move back another fifty yards, and then another fifty yards, and then another. My face hurt. I would never have dreamed that a bonfire could make that much heat, not even one that was three stories high.

Once people had retreated to a sufficient distance, a sense of happy fascination returned, and when the ornamental top of the tower was consumed by the fire, the crowd applauded. The ornament at the summit had been built to resemble a little house, and now the house contained a miniature inferno. This and the vague sense of danger and the heat all disturbed me somehow, and I could not seem to share the feeling of a festive occasion. Instead, perversely, I began to think about the reality of the witch burnings in the sixteenth and seventeenth centuries, events I have always thought of as incomprehensible, and hot as I was, I shivered a little. It is one thing to read about a fire large enough to execute a human being. It is another thing to stand in front of such a fire, along with an excited, hooting crowd. The sinister historical associations would not leave me, and stubbornly kept me from taking any delight in the moment.

I wondered: How had the witch burnings happened? How could such nightmares have been real? Ever the psychologist, I looked around at the people. Clearly, these were not bewildered Basque refugees in 1610, frantically searching for diabolists to burn. Here we were, a crowd of new-millennium, peace-loving, nonhysterical citizens, unscarred by hardship or menacing superstition. There was no blood lust here, or subjugation of conscience. There was laughter and neighborly feeling. We were eating hot dogs and drinking Slurpees and celebrating Independence Day. We were not a heartless, amoral mob, and we would by no means have rallied around a murder, let alone the staging of a torture. If by some bizarre reality warp there had suddenly been a human figure writhing in those colossal flames, only the anonymous handful of sociopaths among us would have been unaffected or perhaps entertained. Of the rest, a few good people would have stared in paralyzed disbelief, a number of especially courageous people would have tried to intervene, and most of the crowd would have fled in understandable terror. And the once-cheerful bonfire would have become a traumatic image seared into all of our brains for the rest of our lives.

But what if the burning human figure had been Osama bin Laden? How would this crowd of American nationals in 2002 have reacted if suddenly confronted with the public execution of the person identified by them as the world's most despicable villain? Would these normally conscience-bound, churchgoing, nonviolent people have stood by and allowed it? Might there have been enthusiasm, or at least acquiescence, rather than nausea and horror at the spectacle of a human being dying in agony?

Standing there among all those good people, I suddenly realized that the reaction might have been something less than horror, simply because Osama bin Laden is *not* a human being in our view. He is Osama, and as such, to borrow an expression from Ervin Staub in *The Roots of Evil,* he has been completely "excluded from our moral universe." The interventions of conscience no longer apply to him. He is not human. He is an *it.* And unfortunately, this transformation of a man into an *it* makes him scarier as well.

Sometimes people appear to deserve our moral exclusion of them, as terrorists appear to do. Other examples of *its* are war criminals, child abductors, and serial killers, and in each of these cases, a considered argument can be (and has been) made, rightly or wrongly, that certain rights to compassionate treatment have been forfeited. But in most cases, our tendency to reduce people to non-beings is neither considered nor conscious, and throughout history our proclivity to dehumanize has too often been turned against the essentially innocent. The list of out groups that some portion of humankind has at one time or another demoted to the status of hardly even human is extremely long and, ironically, includes categories for nearly every one of us: blacks, Communists, capitalists, gays, Native Americans, Jews, foreigners, "witches," women, Muslims, Christians, the Palestinians, the Israelis, the poor, the rich, the Irish, the English, the Americans, the Sinhalese, Tamils, Albanians, Croats, Serbs, Hutus, Tutsis, and Iraqis, to name but a few.

And once the other group has become populated by *its,* anything goes, especially if someone in authority gives the order. Conscience is no longer necessary, because conscience binds us to other beings and not to *its*. Conscience still exists, may even be very exacting, but it applies only to my countrymen, my friends, and my children, not yours. You are excluded from my moral universe, and with impunity—and maybe even praise from the others in my group—I can now drive you from your home, or shoot your family, or burn you alive.

I should record that nothing bad actually happened at the bonfire in 2002. As far as I know, these macabre thoughts occurred only to me. The flames consumed only wood. The fire was a sight to behold, and then burned itself out, just as planned. Laughing children, safe in their hometown, romped on the beach and got doused by the firemen. One wishes that human gatherings could always be as peaceful.

The Emperor's New Clothes

When conscience falls into a profound trance, when it sleeps through acts of torture, war, and genocide, political leaders and other prominent individuals can make the difference between a gradual reawakening of our seventh sense and a continued amoral nightmare. History teaches that attitudes and plans coming from the top dealing pragmatically with problems of hardship and insecurity in the group, rather than scapegoating an out group, can help us return to a more realistic view of the "others." In time, moral leadership can make a difference. But history shows us also that a leader with no seventh sense can hypnotize the group conscience still further, redoubling catastrophe. Using fear-based propaganda to amplify a destructive ideology, such a leader can bring the members of a frightened society to see the *its* as the sole impediment to the good life, for themselves and maybe even for humanity as a whole, and the conflict as an epic battle between good and evil. Once these beliefs have been disseminated, crushing the *its* without pity or conscience can, with chilling ease, become an incontrovertible mandate.

The recurrence throughout history of this second type of leader raises a long list of dumbfounding questions. Why does the human race tolerate this sorrowful story over and over, like a mindless broken record? Why do we continue to allow leaders who are motivated by self-interest, or by their own psychological issues from the past, to fan bitterness and political crisis into armed confrontation and war? In the worst instances, why do we let people who think like frog-killing, arm-breaking Skip run the show and play games of dominance with other people's lives? What becomes of our individual consciences? Why do we not stand up for what we feel?

One explanation is our trancelike state, which lets us believe that the ones who are dying are only *its* anyway. And there is fear, of course—always—and often a sense of helplessness. We look around at the crowd and we think to ourselves, Too many are against me, or I don't hear any other people protesting this, or, even more resignedly, That's just the way the world is, or That's politics. All of these feelings and beliefs can significantly mute our moral sense, but where the disabling of conscience by authority is concerned, there is something even more effective, something more elemental than objectifying the "others," more cloying and miserable than a sense of helplessness, and evidently more difficult to conquer than fear itself. Very simply, we are programmed to obey authority *even against our own consciences.*

In 1961 and 1962, in New Haven, Connecticut, Yale University professor Stanley Milgram designed and filmed one of the most astonishing psychological experiments ever conducted. Milgram set out to pit the human tendency to obey authority as squarely as possible against individual conscience. Concerning his method of inquiry, he wrote, "Of all moral principles, the one that comes closest to being universally accepted is this: one should not inflict suffering on a helpless person who is neither harmful nor threatening to oneself. This principle is the counterforce we shall set in opposition to obedience."

Milgram's experimental procedure was relentlessly straightforward, and the filmed version of his study has outraged humanists, and unsuspecting college students, for forty years. In the study, two men, strangers to each other, arrive at a psychology laboratory to participate in an experiment that has been advertised as having to do with memory and learning. Participation is rewarded with four dollars, plus fifty cents for carfare. At the lab, the experimenter (Stanley Milgram himself, in the filmed version) explains to both men that the study concerns "the effects of punishment on learning." One of the two is designated as the "learner" and is escorted into another room and seated in a chair. All watch as the learner's arms are matter-of-factly strapped to the chair, "to prevent excessive movement," and an electrode is attached to his wrist. He is told that he must learn a list of word pairs (*blue box, nice day, wild duck,* etc.), and that whenever he makes a mistake, he will receive an electric shock. With each mistake, the shock will increase in intensity.

The other person is told that he is to be the "teacher" in this learning experiment. After the teacher has watched the learner get strapped to a chair and wired for electric shock, the teacher is taken into a different room and asked to take a seat in front of a large, ominous machine called a "shock generator." The shock generator has thirty switches, arranged horizontally and labeled by "volts," from 15 volts all the way to 450 volts, in 15-volt increments. In addition to the numbers, the switches are branded with descriptors that range from SLIGHT SHOCK to the sinister appellation of DANGER—SEVERE SHOCK. The teacher is handed the list of word pairs and told that his job is to administer a test to the learner in the other room. When the learner gets an answer right—for example, teacher calls out "blue," and learner answers "box"—the teacher can move on to the next test item. But when the learner gives an incorrect answer, the teacher must push a switch and give him an electric shock. The experimenter instructs the teacher to begin at the lowest level of shock on the shock generator, and with each wrong answer, to increase the shock level by one increment.

The learner in the other room is actually the experimenter's trained confederate, an actor, and will receive no shocks at all. But of course the teacher does not know this, and it is the teacher who is the real subject of the experiment.

The teacher calls out the first few items of the "learning test," and then trouble begins, because the learner—Milgram's accomplice, unseen in the other room—starts to sound very uncomfortable. At 75 volts, the learner makes a mistake on the word pair, the teacher administers the shock, and the learner grunts. At 120 volts, the learner shouts to the experimenter that the shocks are becoming painful, and at 150 volts, the unseen learner demands to be released from the experiment. As the shocks get stronger, the learner's protests sound more and more desperate, and at 285 volts, he emits an agonized scream. The experimenter—the Yale professor in the white lab coat—stands behind the teacher, who is seated at the shock generator, and calmly gives a sequence of scripted prods, such as "Please continue," or "The experiment requires that you continue," or "Whether the learner likes it or not, you must go on until he has learned all the word pairs correctly. So please go on."

Milgram repeated this procedure forty times using forty different subjects—people who were "in everyday life responsible and decent"—including high school teachers, postal clerks, salesmen, manual laborers, and engineers. The forty represented various educational levels, from one man who had not finished high school to others who had doctoral or other professional degrees. The aim of the experiment was to discover how long the subjects (the teachers in this experiment) would take to disobey Milgram's authority when presented with a clear moral imperative. How much electric shock would they administer to a pleading, screaming stranger merely because an authority figure told them to do so?

When I show Milgram's film to a lecture hall full of psychology students, I ask them to predict the answers to these questions. The students are always certain that conscience will prevail. Many of them predict that a large number of the subjects will walk out of the experiment as soon as they find out about the use of electric shock. Most of the students are sure that, of the subjects who remain, all but a few will defy the experimenter, perhaps telling him to go to hell, at least by the time the man in the other room demands to be freed (at 150 volts). And of course, the students predict, only a tiny number of very sick, sadistic subjects will continue pushing switches all the way to 450 volts, where the machine itself says DANGER—SEVERE SHOCK.

Here is what actually happens: Thirty-four of Milgram's original forty subjects continue to shock the learner, whom they believe to be strapped to a chair, even after he asks to be released from the experiment. In fact, of these thirty-four subjects, twenty-five—that is to say, 62.5 percent of the total group—never disobey the experimenter at any point, continuing to press the switches all the way to the end of the sequence (450 volts) despite entreaties and shrieks from the man in the other room. The teachers sweat, they complain, they hold their heads, but they continue. When the film is over, I watch the clock. In a lecture hall full of students who have just seen this experiment for the first time, there is always stunned silence for at least one full minute.

After the original experiment, Milgram varied his design in a number of ways. In one variation, for example, subjects were not commanded to operate the switches that shocked the learner, only to call out the words for the word-pair test before another person pushed the switches. In this version of the experiment, thirty-seven of forty people (92.5 percent) continued to participate to the highest shock level on the "generator." Thus far, the teachers in the study had been only men. Milgram now tried his experiment using forty women, speculating that women might be more empathic. Their performance was virtually identical, except that obedient women reported more stress than obedient men. Studies using the Milgram model were repeated at several other universities, and soon involved more than a thousand subjects of both genders and from many walks of life. The results remained essentially the same.

The many-times-replicated outcome of his obedience study led Milgram to make the famous pronouncement that has haunted, and also motivated, so many students of human nature: "A substantial proportion of people do what they are told to do, irrespective of the content of the act and without limitations of conscience, so long as they perceive that the command comes from a legitimate authority." Milgram believed that authority could put conscience to sleep mainly because the obedient person makes an "adjustment of thought," which is to see himself as *not responsible for his own actions.*

In his mind, he is no longer a person who must act in a morally accountable way, but the agent of an external authority to whom he attributes all responsibility and all initiative. This "adjustment of thought" makes it much easier for benign leadership to establish order and control, but by the same psychological mechanism, it has countless times rolled out the red carpet for self-serving, malevolent, and sociopathic "authorities."

Where Conscience Draws the Line

The extent to which authority dulls conscience is affected by the perceived legitimacy of that authority. If the person giving the orders is seen as a subordinate, or even as an equal, the same "adjustment of thought" may never occur. In Milgram's initial study, one of the minority of people who eventually refused to continue with the experiment was a thirty-two-year-old engineer who apparently regarded the scientist in the lab coat as, at most, his intellectual peer. This subject pushed his chair away from the shock generator and in an indignant tone said to Milgram, "I'm an electrical engineer, and I have had shocks . . . I think I've gone too far already, probably." In an interview later, when Milgram asked him who was accountable for shocking the man in the other room, he did not assign any responsibility to the experimenter. Instead, he replied, "I would put it on myself entirely." He was a professional person with an advanced education, and education must be acknowledged as one of the factors that determine whether or not conscience stays alert. It would be a grave and arrogant mistake to imagine that an academic degree directly increases the strength of conscience in the human psyche. On the other hand, education can sometimes level the perceived legitimacy of an authority figure, and thereby limit unquestioning obedience. With education and knowledge, the individual may be able to hold on to the perception of him- or herself as a legitimate authority.

Relatedly, in another permutation of his experiment, Milgram posed an "ordinary man," rather than a scientist, as the person who ordered the subjects to administer shocks. When an "ordinary man" was in charge, instead of a man in a white lab coat, obedience on the part of the subjects dropped from 62.5 percent to 20 percent. Packaging and perceptions are not everything, but evidently they get pretty close. Some of us may resist a person who looks like we do, but most of us will obey someone who *looks like* an authority. This finding is of particular concern in an age when our leaders and experts come to us via the magic of television, where nearly anyone can be made to appear patrician and commandingly larger than life.

In addition to being larger than life, images on television are up close and personal—they are in our living rooms—and another factor that affects authority's power to overwhelm individual conscience is the proximity of the person giving the commands. When Milgram varied his experiment such that he was not in the room, obedience dropped by two-thirds, to about the same level as when an "ordinary man" was in charge. And when authority was not close by, subjects tended to "cheat" by using only the lower shock levels on the machine.

The nearness of authority is especially relevant to the real-life obedience requirements of combat and war. As it turns out, individual conscience draws a surprisingly firm line at killing—surprising for those who think of human beings as natural war makers. This aspect of conscience is so resilient in normal people that military psychologists have needed to devise ways around it. For example, military experts now know that to make men kill with any kind of reliability, commands must be given by authorities who are present with the troops. Otherwise, the men in the field will tend to "cheat" on their orders to kill, will intentionally misaim or simply fail to fire, to keep from violating this mightiest proscription of conscience.

Brig. Gen. S. L. A Marshall was a United States combat historian in the Pacific theater during World War II and later became the official historian of the European theater of operations. He wrote of many World War II incidents in which almost all soldiers obeyed and fired their weapons while their leaders were present to command them, but when the leaders left, the firing rate dropped immediately to between 15 and 20 percent. Marshall believed that the great relief displayed by soldiers in a sector where they were not being directly ordered to fire "was due not so much to the realization that things were safer there as to the blessed knowledge that for a time they were *not under the compulsion to take life.*"

In his book *On Killing: The Psychological Cost of Learning to Kill in War and Society,* former U.S. Army Ranger and paratrooper Lt. Col. Dave Grossman reviews Marshall's observations, along with the FBI's studies of nonfiring rates among law-enforcement officers in the 1950s and 1960s, and observations of nonfiring from a long list of wars, including the American Civil War, World Wars I and II, the Vietnam War, and the Falklands War. He concludes that "the vast majority of combatants throughout history, at the moment of truth when they could and should kill the enemy, have found themselves to be 'conscientious objectors.' " After weighing the considerable historical evidence that ground soldiers often resist and quietly sabotage opportunities to kill, Grossman comes to a "novel and reassuring conclusion about the nature of man: despite an unbroken tradition of violence and war, man is not by nature a killer." To subvert the bottom line of conscience, to be able to thrust a bayonet or pull a trigger to kill a stranger, normal human beings must be carefully taught, psychologically conditioned, and commanded by authorities on the battlefield.

Also, it helps to encourage moral exclusion, to remind the troops that the enemy soldiers are nothing but *its,* Krauts, slants, gooks. As Peter Watson writes in *War on the Mind: The Military Uses and Abuses of Psychology,* "the stupidity of local customs is ridiculed," and "local personalities are presented as evil demigods."

On and off the battlefield, for both the troops and the people back home, the particular war being fought must be portrayed as a crucial or even a sacred struggle between good and evil, which is exactly the message that authorities—on all sides of the conflict—have tried to convey during every major war in history. For example, though it is now difficult to remember anything but the moral outrage that exploded during the final phases of the Vietnam War, as that war began, Americans were repeatedly assured that they and only they could save the South Vietnamese people from a future of terror and enslavement. Speeches by leaders during wartime, in modern times broadcasted into our living rooms, have always pushed hard on this theme of an absolutely necessary mission, the high calling that justifies the killing. And paradoxically, authority can more readily project this take on reality for the very reason that conscience cherishes a high calling and a sense of membership in the right-minded group. In other words, conscience can be tricked, and when it comes to killing strangers, trickery is usually required.

That psychology can provide the military with techniques to make killers out of nonkillers, and that the military is using these procedures, is dispiriting news. But behind the bad news is a particle of hope that glints like a diamond in a sea of darkness. We are beginning to learn that human beings are not the natural killing machines we have at times believed ourselves to be. Even under the desperate pressures of combat, we have often left our weapons unfired, or taken poor aim, for when it was not silenced under the bell jar of authority, there was always an outcry from our human connectedness—there has always been the voice of conscience—reminding us that we must not kill.

Because its essence is killing, war is the ultimate contest between conscience and authority. Our seventh sense demands that we not take life, and when authority overrules conscience and a soldier is induced to kill in combat, he is very likely to suffer post-traumatic stress disorder immediately and for the remainder of his life, along with the depression, divorces, addictions, ulcers, and heart disease that attend traumatic memory. In contrast, research involving Vietnam veterans has shown that soldiers who are not placed in situations where they are forced to kill are no more likely to develop the symptoms of PTSD than are those who spend their entire enlistment at home.

This crippling competition between our moral sense and our authority figures has gone on almost unceasingly since human beings began to live in hierarchical societies, for the past five thousand years during which a king or a land-hungry nobleman, or the leader of a state or a nation could order less powerful individuals to enter a battle and kill. And apparently it is a struggle of conscience that will not be resolved in our children's or our grandchildren's lifetimes.

Obedience 6, Conscience 4

Stanley Milgram, who demonstrated that at least six out of ten people will tend to obey to the bitter end an official-looking authority who is physically present, pointed out that people who disobey destructive authority suffer psychologically, too. Often a person who disobeys finds himself at odds with the social order, and may find it hard to shake the feeling that he has been faithless to someone or something to whom he pledged allegiance. Obedience is passive, and it is only the disobedient one who must bear the "burden of his action," to use Milgram's words. If courage is acting according to one's conscience despite pain or fear, then strength is the ability to keep conscience awake and in force despite the demands of authorities to do otherwise.

And strength is important, because in championing the various causes of conscience, the odds are against us.

To illustrate, I propose an imaginary society of exactly one hundred adults, in a group that conforms precisely to known statistics. This means that of the one hundred people in my hypothetical society, four are sociopathic—they have no conscience. Of the remaining ninety-six decent citizens, all of whom do have consciences, 62.5 percent will obey authority more or less without question, quite possibly the authority of one of the more aggressive and controlling sociopaths in the crowd. This leaves thirty-six people who have both conscience and the strength to bear the burdens of their actions, a little more than a third of the group. These are not impossible odds, but they are not easy ones, either.

And there is yet another challenge for the conscience-bound, which is that, strange as it seems, most of the sociopaths are invisible. Let us turn to that dilemma now, and the remarkable case of Doreen Littlefield.

FOUR

the nicest person in the world

I saw a werewolf drinking a piña colada at Trader Vic's
His hair was perfect

—*Warren Zevon*

Doreen glances in the rearview mirror and wishes for the billionth time that she were beautiful. Life would be so much easier. She appears pretty in the mirror this morning, rested and with all of her makeup on, but she knows that if she were not so skilled with the cosmetics, or if she were tired, she would look quite plain. She would look plain like the unsophisticated girl from the sticks that she was, more as if she belonged milking a cow than in the driver's seat of this black BMW. She is only thirty-four, and her skin still looks good, no lines yet, a little pale maybe. But her nose is slightly pointed, enough to be noticeable, and her straw-colored hair, her most problematic feature, stays dry and frizzled no matter what she does to it. Luckily, her body is excellent. She looks away from the mirror and down at her light gray silk suit, conservative but formfitting. Doreen's body is good, and even better, she knows just how to move. For a woman with a plain face, she is incredibly seductive.

When she walks across a room, all the men in it watch. Remembering this, she smiles and starts the car.

About a mile from her apartment, she realizes that she forgot to feed the damn Maltese. Oh well. The stupid froufrou dog will manage to survive until she gets home from work tonight. At this point, a month after the impulse purchase, she cannot believe she ever bought it anyway. She had thought she would look elegant when she walked it, but walking it turned out to be tedious. When she can find the time, she will have to get it put to sleep, or maybe she can sell it to someone. It was expensive, after all.

In her parking area on the sprawling grounds of the psychiatric hospital, she makes sure to park her car beside Jenna's rusted-out Escort, a convenient visual comparison to remind Jenna of their relative places in the world. One more glance in the mirror and then Doreen picks up her briefcase, stuffed to overflowing to make it clear how hard she works, and walks up the stairs to the suite of offices above the ward. As she passes through the waiting room, she flashes a "We're good buddies" smile at Ivy, the frumpy secretary-receptionist for the unit, and Ivy immediately brightens.

"Good morning, Dr. Littlefield. Oh my goodness, I love your suit! It's just gorgeous!"

"Why, thank you, Ivy. I can always count on you to put me in a good mood," Doreen replies with another big smile. "Buzz me when my patient gets here, would you?"

Doreen disappears into her office, and Ivy shakes her head and says out loud to an empty waiting room, "That has got to be the nicest person in the world."

It is early, not quite eight o'clock, and in her office Doreen goes to the window to watch her colleagues arrive. She sees Jackie Rubenstein walking toward the building, with her long legs and her effortless posture. Jackie is from Los Angeles, even-tempered and funny, and her beautiful olive skin makes her look, always, as if she just got back from a wonderful vacation. She is brilliant as well, a great deal smarter than Doreen, and for this reason even more than the others, Doreen secretly despises her. In fact, she hates her so much that she would kill her if she thought she could get away with it, but she knows she would eventually get caught. Doreen and Jackie were postdocs together at the hospital eight years ago, became friends, at least in Jackie's eyes, and now Doreen is hearing rumors that Jackie may receive the Mentor of the Year Award. They are the same age. How can Jackie possibly win an award for being a "mentor" at the age of thirty-four?

From the lawn, Jackie Rubenstein looks up and notices Doreen in the office window. She waves. Doreen smiles girlishly and waves back.

At this moment, Ivy buzzes Doreen for her first patient of the day, a stunningly handsome, broad-shouldered, but very frightened-looking young man named Dennis. In hospital lingo, Dennis is a VIP (very important patient), because he is the nephew of a famous national politician. In this major teaching hospital, there are a number of such VIPs, celebrities, the wealthy, family members of people whose names are household words. Dennis is not one of Doreen's psychotherapy patients. Rather, Doreen is his administrator, which means that she meets with him twice a week to inquire how his treatment is going, to make sure the paperwork is done, and to approve his discharge from the hospital when the time comes. Doreen has already heard from the staff that today Dennis will want to discuss his release. He thinks he has gotten better enough to go home.

To separate the administrative tasks from the psychotherapeutic ones is hospital policy. Each patient has both an administrator and a therapist. Dennis's therapist, whom he worships, is the talented Dr. Jackie Rubenstein. Yesterday, Jackie told Doreen that her patient Dennis was tremendously improved, and that she plans to take him on as an outpatient when he leaves the hospital.

Now Dennis sits in one of the low chairs in Doreen Littlefield's office and tries to make eye contact, as he knows he should if he is going to appear well enough to go home from the hospital. But he has a hard time and keeps looking away. Something about her gray suit scares him, and something about her eyes. Still, he likes her, he thinks. She has always been extremely nice to him, and other people have told him that of all the doctors, Dr. Littlefield is the one who is most interested in the patients. Anyway, she is the expert.

Doreen, seated behind her desk, looks at Dennis and marvels again at the perfect lines of his face and his muscular twenty-six-year-old body. She wonders how much money he will end up inheriting. But then she remembers her mission, and tries to lock in his nervous gaze with a maternal smile.

"I hear you've been feeling much better this week, Dennis."

"That's right, Dr. Littlefield. I've been feeling much better this week. Really, a whole lot better. My ideas are much better. They're not bothering me all the time like they were when I came in."

"Why do you think that is, Dennis? Why do you think they're not bothering you anymore?"

"Oh, well, I've really been working hard on the cognitive therapy techniques Dr. Rubenstein taught me, you know? They're okay. I mean, they help. And . . . Well, the thing is, I think I'm ready to go home now. Or soon maybe? Dr. Rubenstein said she could keep seeing me as an outpatient."

Dennis's "ideas," the ones that are not bothering him so much at present, are the paranoid delusions that completely take over his life from time to time. Once a vibrant teenager who made stellar grades and was the champion of his high school lacrosse team, Dennis suffered a psychotic breakdown during his freshman year in college and was hospitalized. In the seven years since then, he has been in and out of psychiatric facilities as his delusions waxed and waned but never really left him. When these terrifying "ideas" have him in their grip, he believes that people are trying to kill him and lying about their intentions, that the streetlights are monitoring his thoughts for the CIA, that every passing car contains an agent who has been sent to abduct and question him for crimes that he cannot remember. His sense of reality is fragile in the extreme, and the torment of his suspiciousness, which is present even when the concrete delusions are in remission, makes it increasingly difficult for him to be around other people, even therapists. Jackie Rubenstein has done an almost miraculous job of forging a therapeutic relationship with this lonely young man who trusts no one.

"You say Dr. Rubenstein said you could be discharged, and that she'd see you as an outpatient?"

"Yes. Yes, that was what she suggested. I mean, she agreed that I was almost ready to go home."

"Really?" Doreen looks at Dennis with a puzzled expression on her face, as if expecting some clarification. "That's not what she told me."

There is a long pause, during which Dennis shudders visibly. Finally, he asks, "What do you mean?"

Doreen emits a stage sigh, full of compassion, and comes out from behind her desk to sit in the chair beside Dennis's. She tries to put her hand on his shoulder, but he pulls his body away from her, as if she were about to strike him. Staring out the window as far into the distance as he can, he repeats his question, "What do you mean that's not what she told you?"

Doreen understands enough about paranoid schizophrenia to know that Dennis already suspects this is going to be news of treachery on the part of Dr. Rubenstein, the person he thought was his only real friend in the world.

"What Dr. Rubenstein told me was that she was sure you were much sicker now than when you came in. And as for outpatient therapy, she made it very clear that she'd never agree to see you outside of the hospital. She said you were much too dangerous."

Even to Doreen, it is apparent that something in Dennis's heart is flying out of the window and away, not to return to him anytime soon. She says, "Dennis? Dennis, are you okay?"

Dennis does not move or speak.

She tries again. "I'm so sorry I had to be the one to tell you this. Dennis? I'm sure it was just a misunderstanding. You know Dr. Rubenstein would never lie to you."

But Dennis is silent. He has to cope with the fear of betrayal every minute of his life, but this huge new wave of it, coming from his wonderful Dr. Rubenstein, has blindsided him and made him stone-still, like a statue.

When Doreen realizes that he really is not going to respond at all, she goes to the phone and calls for assistance. In no time, two burly mental health workers appear at her office door. They are big, but she is the authority, and they will obey her orders without question. Thinking this gives her a little shiver of pleasure, but wearing her gravest expression, she signs the order to board Dennis. "Boarding"—a euphemism that makes it sound like the hospital is putting someone up at an inn—means that a patient is transferred from an unlocked ward, such as the one Dennis has been in, to a locked unit with greater security. Patients are boarded if they become violent, or when, like Dennis, they have had a serious relapse. If necessary, they are restrained and remedicated.

Doreen is fairly certain that Dennis will not tell anyone about what she has just said to him. Dennis does not tell his secrets. He is too paranoid. But even if he does tell someone, he will not be believed. No one ever believes the patients over the doctors. And from what she just saw, he will be out of it for quite a long time, and not really talking about anything. With a rush of satisfaction, she realizes that Jackie Rubenstein has just lost herself one truly delectable VIP patient. He will be wildly paranoid about Jackie now, and the best part is that Jackie will blame herself, will think she missed something important in her therapy with him, or said something harmful. Jackie is such a loser about things like that. She will actually take the rap, and then she will hand the patient off to another therapist. So much for all the talk around the hospital about Dr. Rubenstein being a miracle worker.

Blue Smoke and Mirrors

Doreen Littlefield is what personality theorist Theodore Millon would call a "covetous psychopath," where "psychopath" refers to sociopathy, or the absence of conscience, and "covetous" has its usual referent: an inordinate desire for the possessions of others. Sociopaths do not always have a covetous nature—some are very differently motivated—but when lack of conscience and covetousness occur together in the same individual, a fascinating and frightening picture emerges. Since it is simply not possible to steal and have for oneself the most valuable "possessions" of another person—beauty, intelligence, success, a strong character—the covetous sociopath settles for besmirching or damaging enviable qualities in others so that they will not have them, either, or at least not be able to enjoy them so much. As Millon says, "Here, the pleasure lies in taking rather than in having."

The covetous sociopath thinks that life has cheated her somehow, has not given her nearly the same bounty as other people, and so she must even the existential score by robbing people, by secretly causing destruction in other lives. She believes she has been slighted by nature, circumstances, and destiny, and that diminishing other people is her only means of being powerful. Retribution, usually against people who have no idea that they have been targeted, is the most important activity in the covetous sociopath's life, her highest priority.

Since this clandestine power game is priority number one, all of the covetous sociopath's deceitfulness and tolerance for risk are devoted to it. For the sake of the game, she may devise schemes and perform acts that most of us would consider outrageous and potentially self-destructive, in addition to cruel. And yet when such a person is around us in our lives, even on a daily basis, we are often oblivious to her activities. We do not expect to see a person direct a dangerous, vicious vendetta against someone who in most cases has done nothing to hurt or offend her. We do not expect it, and so we do not see it, even when it happens to someone we know—or to us personally. The actions taken by the covetous sociopath are often so outlandish, and so gratuitously mean, that we refuse to believe they were intentional, or even that they happened at all. In this way, her true nature is usually invisible to the group. She can easily hide in plain sight, as Doreen has done among genuinely intelligent, professional people at the hospital for nearly a decade.

The covetous sociopath is the ultimate wolf in sheep's clothing, and in Doreen's case, the disguise is especially elaborate. Doreen is a psychologist, or, at any rate, everyone at the hospital believes she is a psychologist, which for Doreen Littlefield's purposes is much the same thing. The truth, should anyone ever discover it, is that she has no psychology license, nor does she have a doctoral degree. When she was twenty-two, she did receive a bachelor's degree in psychology from her state university back home, but that is all. The rest is an extravagant charade. When they hired her as a postdoc at the hospital, they checked her references, but these were both very prominent men who had succumbed to certain embarrassing liaisons with her, though they should have known better. The hiring committee did not check the credentials she listed. Because she came so prestigiously recommended, they simply assumed she had a Ph.D. After all, who on earth would lie about a thing like that? As for her ability to behave like a psychologist well enough to fool the professionals and the patients, Doreen has always felt, and apparently she is borne out in this opinion, that a person can learn a lot by reading books.

Doreen has just seen her recovering eight o'clock patient, drop-kicked him into an acutely paranoid state as retribution against an innocent colleague, and sent him off to be medicated and confined to a locked unit. What does she do for the remainder of the day? If we were to rejoin her in her office, we would find that she calmly meets with the rest of her scheduled patients, makes phone calls, does paperwork, and goes to a staff meeting. We would probably not see anything out of the ordinary. Most of her behavior would look normal to us, or close enough to pass. Perhaps she does not do her patients very much good, but she does them no obvious harm either, except in those instances, like this morning, when manipulating a patient will serve to damage a colleague she has targeted.

Why would she direct her skills against psychiatric inpatients? They have nothing she wants. They are disenfranchised by the world, and she can feel powerful merely by sitting in a room with them. The exception might be the occasional female patient who is a little too attractive or, worse, a little too smart. Then Doreen might have to bring her down a peg or two, tweak a bit of the self-hatred that is usually already there in these patients. In her role as a psychotherapist, she finds this ridiculously easy to do. The setup is always one-on-one, and the patient never understands what hit her well enough to complain to anyone outside of the therapy room.

But when people do not provoke in Doreen a desire for something they have, or for something they *are,* then she does not target them. To the contrary, she may be especially charming and courteous when she believes that certain underlings, as she thinks of them, are useful in maintaining her sheep's-clothing disguise, a disguise that includes a presentation of herself as an extraordinarily nice, caring, responsible, and pitiably overworked person. For example, when Doreen is preparing to leave work on the day she has secretly sabotaged Jackie Rubenstein and Dennis, she makes sure to stop by Ivy's desk for an endearing little chat. She tries to do this every evening. Ivy is the secretary-receptionist for the professionals on the ward, and one never knows when such a strategically placed person may come in handy.

Doreen comes out of her office, collapses into one of the reception room chairs, and says, "Oh Ivy! I'm so grateful this day is over!"

Ivy is twenty years older than Doreen. She is overweight and wears big plastic earrings. Doreen thinks she is pathetic.

Ivy replies to her warmly, "I know. You poor thing. And that poor Dennis! I'm no doctor, but I do see the patients around, you know, and I sort of had my hopes up. . . . I guess I was wrong."

"No, no. You're very observant. He did seem better for a while. This work breaks your heart sometimes."

Of course, this morning the two no-nonsense attendants carrying Dennis off the ward passed right in front of a wide-eyed Ivy. She now looks at Doreen with concern.

"You know, Dr. Littlefield, I worry about you."

As Ivy makes this confession, she notices that Doreen's eyes are pooling with tears, and she continues in a lower voice, "Oh my, today was terrible for you, wasn't it, dear? I hope you won't think I'm getting too personal, but you're so sensitive to be doing this kind of work."

"No, no, Ivy. I'm just tired, and of course I'm sad about Dennis. Don't tell anyone—I'm not supposed to play favorites—but he's special to me, you know? I wish I could just go home and get a good night's sleep."

"Well, that's exactly what you should do, dear."

"I wish I could, but what with the emergency and all, I didn't get my paperwork done, and I think I'm going to be up half the night doing it."

Ivy glances at Doreen's bulging briefcase and says, "You poor thing. Let's think of something nice, maybe, to get your mind off . . . well, what happened today. How's that new Maltese doggy of yours?"

Doreen blots her eyes with the back of her hand and smiles. "Oh, he's terrific, Ivy. Actually, sometimes he's so cute I could just eat him up."

Ivy chuckles. "Well then, I'll bet he's waiting for you. Why don't you go on home now and give him a great big hug?"

"Better not be too big. I'll squish him. He's teeny."

The two women laugh together over this, and then Doreen says, "Ivy, Ivy. You know, I think you should be the psychologist. You always know how to put me in a better mood. I'll see you bright and early tomorrow, okay? We'll just keep on keeping on, I guess."

"I'll be here," affirms Ivy. She beams as Doreen picks up her briefcase and walks away, listing a bit to the briefcase side.

Doreen walks back to the lot where she left her car, and there she encounters Jenna, owner of the beat-up Escort she parked beside this morning. Jenna is a new intern at the hospital, and, unlike Ivy the receptionist, she is young, bright, and pretty. She has long, lovely, stick-straight auburn hair, and Doreen has targeted her.

"Hello, Jenna. Going home?"

Jenna blinks at the obvious question, which she thinks is probably criticism, since interns are expected to work slavishly long hours. But she recoups. "Yeah. Yes. Going home. You, too?"

Doreen looks concerned. "What about that emergency conference at Chatwin Hall?"

Chatwin Hall houses a ward directed by the stern and fearsome Dr. Thomas Larson, whom Doreen knows to be Jenna's primary supervisor. There is, of course, no conference there right now. Doreen has made this up on the spot.

Jenna turns ashen immediately. "There's an emergency conference? Nobody told me. When? Why? Do you know?"

Doreen, now taking on the demeanor of a schoolmarm, looks at her watch and says, "About ten minutes ago, I believe. Didn't you pick up your phone messages?"

"Yes, of course I did, but there really wasn't anything about a conference. Dr. Larson's office?"

"I suppose."

"Oh no. Oh my God. I've got to . . . I should . . . Well, I guess I'll just get there as fast as I can."

"Good idea."

Jenna is too panicked to wonder why Dr. Littlefield knows about a spur-of-the-moment conference that does not even involve her. The young intern dashes out of the parking lot and begins to run in her leather pumps across an acre of rain-soaked hospital lawn. Doreen stands in the parking lot and watches her go until, still sprinting, she makes a turn around the far side of a building and disappears from view. Reflecting in satisfaction that Chatwin Hall is located on the extreme opposite end of the grounds, Doreen gets into the BMW, checks her makeup in the rearview mirror, and starts for home. Tomorrow, or the next day, she will come across Jenna again, and Jenna will ask her about the conference that did not exist. Doreen will just shrug and look hard into Jenna's soft eyes, and Jenna will back off.

Sociopathy Versus Criminality

Doreen Littlefield will never be prosecuted for her deeds, including practicing psychology without a license. Dennis's influential uncle will never discover who she really is, nor will most of her other patients or their families. The professionals at the hospital will never pursue her legally for her criminal deception of them. She will never be punished in anything like a commensurate way for the countless psychological assaults she commits. In the end, she is a good illustration of the difference between a sociopath and a criminal, which is, astoundingly, the same thing that separates a naughty three-year-old girl who is seen as well behaved from one who is scolded for taking candy from her mother's purse. The difference, quite simply, is whether or not she gets caught.

And adults getting caught for committing acts without conscience is apparently more the exception than the rule. Since 4 percent of the entire population is sociopathic, one might reasonably think that our prison system is filled to overflowing with sociopaths, to the exclusion of other types of people. But this is not the case. According to Robert Hare and other researchers who test convicts, on average only about 20 percent of prison inmates in the United States are sociopaths. Hare and others are careful to note that this 20 percent of the prison population accounts for more than 50 percent of the "most serious crimes" (extortion, armed robbery, kidnapping, murder) and crimes against the state (treason, espionage, terrorism), but the actual sociopathic head count in prisons, for both men and women, is only about two in ten.

Put differently, most identified criminals are not sociopaths. Rather, they are people with more normal underlying personalities whose behavior is the product of negative social forces such as the drug culture, child abuse, domestic violence, and cross-generational poverty. The statistics mean also that very few sociopathic crimes are ever brought to the attention of our legal system—that very few sociopaths are criminals in the formal sense. The most common sociopathic profile, like Doreen's, involves ongoing deception and camouflage, and only the most flagrant crimes (kidnapping, murder, and so forth) are difficult for a reasonably intelligent sociopath to conceal. Some—by no means all—of the sociopathic armed robbers and kidnappers get caught. The Doreen Littlefields of the world seldom do, and even when they do get caught, in the sense of being found out, they are rarely prosecuted. The result is that most sociopaths are not incarcerated. They are out here in the world with you and me.

In the next chapter, we will discuss the many reasons why people of conscience have so much difficulty "seeing" and dealing effectively with people who have no conscience. These reasons range from the fear tactics used by sociopaths to our own misplaced sense of guilt. But first, let us return to the hospital once more, this time to see Dr. Jackie Rubenstein's miracle, two miracles in fact.

It is now four days after Dennis was boarded to a locked unit, a Sunday, and the hospital grounds are empty except for a small car that travels up the narrow drive to Dennis's building and stops by the front door. Dr. Rubenstein steps out and digs in her coat pocket for the tremendous, almost medieval master key that will let her both in and out of the three-story stone building. Even now, after eight years of work at the hospital, she clutches the heavy passkey in her hand, rather than putting it back in her pocket, after she enters a unit like this one and hears the door lock behind her. She has come to try, one more time, to get her terrified patient Dennis to talk to her. When she walks onto the ward itself—and yet another metal door closes behind her and locks—she sees Dennis sitting on a green vinyl sofa and staring at a television that has not been turned on. He looks up, their eyes meet for a moment, and, to her surprise and relief, he motions for her to come and sit down.

Then the first miracle happens: Dennis talks. He talks and he talks, and he tells Jackie Rubenstein everything Doreen Littlefield said. And the second miracle is that Jackie believes him.

From home that night, she phones Doreen and confronts her. Doreen denies everything, and disdainfully accuses her of being drawn into her patient's paranoia. When Jackie refuses to back down, Doreen warns her that she will be damaging her own career if she goes to anyone else at the hospital with such a wild tale. When she hangs up the phone after talking with Doreen, Jackie calls a good friend back in Los Angeles for support. She tells him, only half kidding, that she thinks she may be losing her mind.

Jackie does not know that Doreen is a fraud, and so from Jackie's perspective, she and Doreen are peers at the hospital. For this reason, Jackie realizes that she will have a hard time pressing her point with the more senior staff. They will assume this is just some kind of dispute between her and Jackie. At worst, like Doreen, they may suggest she is letting her patient's issues become her own. Nonetheless, on the following morning she walks into the office of the director of her unit and tells him what has happened. His gray-bearded face reddens, which Jackie finds curious, since he does not seem to be angry, either at her or at Doreen. She wonders, as she has wondered vaguely before, whether he and Doreen have had an affair.

After he hears Jackie out, the director does not take quite the disdainful approach Doreen did on the phone, but he does respectfully remind Jackie of how easy it is to see elements of credibility in the delusions of intelligent paranoids. He says he very much doubts that anything Dennis told her actually happened, and he expresses the hope that she and Doreen will not carry this disagreement out indefinitely. Such a rift would be bad for the unit. And so, in all important respects, Doreen gets away with what she has done, as usual. The happier news is that Dennis's therapy with Jackie is not permanently disrupted, and he is soon discharged from the hospital.

The end of Doreen Littlefield's charade eventually comes, as it so often does for covetous sociopaths, not with a bang but a whimper, and instigated by someone outside of the system. In Doreen's case, the successful whistle-blower is a consumer advocate who appears twice a month on a local television show called *Buyer Beware*. Six years after Doreen's psychological assault on Dennis, this local celebrity's wife is hospitalized for depression, and, completely by chance, Doreen is assigned as her therapist. Rankled because he believes his wife's therapy is somehow mucking up his marriage, he uses his expertise to investigate Dr. Littlefield, and readily discovers what she is—or rather, what she is not. He at once approaches the business director of the hospital and explains that if the hospital will kick Doreen out immediately, find a new therapist for his wife, and forgive his wife's entire hospital bill, he will not expose Doreen and the hospital on television. He points out quite reasonably that forgiving one bill is a lot less expensive than paying back the hundreds of bills, or worse, that will be brought against the hospital should Doreen's credentials, or the lack thereof, be broadcasted.

Reading the file he is shown, the business director is clear on the concept right away, and on her fortieth birthday, in the middle of eating cake at a little office party organized by Ivy, Doreen is abruptly summoned to the administration building. In the business director's office, the business director, the medical director, and the director of nursing (who wants to be present just because she hates Doreen so much) inform Doreen that security will escort her to her car and then monitor her to make certain she leaves the hospital grounds. Doreen tells the three directors that they are making a big mistake, that the consumer advocate is lying because he does not like her, and that she will sue them.

She drives away, and though she was there for fourteen years, no one at the hospital ever hears from her again. The hospital administration does not pursue the matter, for the obvious reasons of public embarrassment and medical liability, and there is a collective sigh of relief when she simply vanishes. In their private conversations about her, the director of nursing and Jackie Rubenstein speculate that Doreen is somewhere else, in some other state, still practicing psychology.

Most of the people at the hospital have vast quantities of conscience, and so why, when they finally find out about Doreen, do they let her go without a fight, most likely to strike again somewhere else? And why, in a psychiatric hospital, was she so hard to see in the first place? In general, how can any of us live, as we all do, among significant numbers of destructive liars and con artists and fail to confront them, or even notice them? As we are about to see, there are answers to these crucial questions, and also ways we can begin to change our responses to the slippery phenomenon of sociopathy.

FIVE

why conscience is partially blind

It is easy—terribly easy—to shake a man's faith in himself. To take advantage of that to break a man's spirit is devil's work.

—*George Bernard Shaw*

If she had thought she could get away with it, Doreen Littlefield would have run Jackie Rubenstein down with her BMW, rather than merely sabotaging her work. And—more amazing still—if she had crushed or killed Jackie, or anyone else, Doreen would have experienced no guilt or remorse, much less the horror most of us would feel if we ended another person's life. Her blood pressure would not have risen one point, at least not from any negative emotion having to do with the victim. Doreen has no such sense of things, no seventh sense of human connectedness to make her feel sick over the consequences of her actions. For most of us, killing someone would result in shock, followed by life-altering anguish, even if we had not liked that person. For Doreen, such an act, provided she was never caught, would be experienced as winning. This difference between normal emotional functioning and sociopathy is almost too fantastic for those of us with conscience to grasp, and so for the most part, we refuse to believe such a hollowness of emotion can exist. And unfortunately, our difficulty in crediting the magnitude of this difference places us in peril.

Even without murdering anyone with her car, or her own two hands, Doreen causes untold damage to the people around her. In fact, diminishing other lives is her primary goal. Since she uses the authority trappings of an inpatient psychotherapist, one day, as a side effect of the vengeful campaigns she conducts, she may push a patient into suicide, if she has not done so already. And yet for fourteen years, a large group of good people, the members of an entire psychiatric hospital staff who would spend their last ounce of strength attempting to prevent a patient's suicide, are blind to what she is, and when they discover her deception, they do not try to stop her. They simply watch her drive away.

Why are conscience-bound human beings so blind? And why are they so hesitant to defend themselves, and the ideals and people they care about, from the minority of human beings who possess no conscience at all? A large part of the answer has to do with the emotions and thought processes that occur in us when we are confronted with sociopathy. We are afraid, and our sense of reality suffers. We think we are imagining things, or exaggerating, or that we ourselves are somehow responsible for the sociopath's behavior. But before we discuss in detail our own psychological reactions to shamelessness, allow me to put these reactions in context by clearly describing what we are up against. Let us first take a careful look at the formidable techniques used by the shameless to keep us in line.

The Tools of the Trade

The first such technique is charm, and as a social force, charm should not be underestimated.

Doreen could be extremely charming when it suited her purposes. Our old friend Skip used his considerable charm to influence his business associates and to grease the fast track to corporate dominance. And charm—though the link may seem counterintuitive—is a primary characteristic of sociopathy. The intense charm of people who have no conscience, a kind of inexplicable charisma, has been observed and commented on by countless victims, and by researchers who attempt to catalog the diagnostic signs of sociopathy. It is a potent characteristic. Most of the victims I have known in my work have reported that their initial involvement with a sociopathic person, and their continued association even though she or he caused them pain, was a direct result of how *charming* she or he could be. Countless times, I have watched people shake their heads and make statements such as, "He was the most charming person I ever met," or "I felt like I'd known her forever," or "He had an energy about him that other people just don't have."

I liken sociopathic charm to the animal charisma of other mammals who are predators. We watch the large cats, for example, and are fascinated with their movements, their independence, and their power. But the direct gaze of a leopard, should one happen to be in the wrong place at the wrong time, is inescapable and tetanizing, and the fascinating charm of the predator is often the last thing the prey ever experiences. (I speak of noble leopards, but I have heard abused and enraged victims use metaphors that were decidedly reptilian.)

Enhancing the animal charisma of sociopaths, there is our own mild affinity for danger. Conventional wisdom has it that dangerous people are attractive, and when we are drawn to sociopaths, we tend to prove out this cliché. Sociopaths are dangerous in many ways. One of the most conspicuous is their preference for risky situations and choices, and their ability to convince others to take risks along with them. On occasion—but only on occasion—normal people enjoy minor risks and thrills. We will get out our wallets and pay for a ride on a monster roller coaster we cannot imagine surviving, or for a seat in a movie theater showing a bloody thriller we are certain will give us bad dreams. Our normal affinity for the occasional thrill can make the risk-taking sociopath seem all the more charming—at first. Initially, it can be exciting to be invited into the risky scheme, to be associated with the person who is making choices outside of our ordinary boundaries.

Let us take your credit card and fly to Paris tonight. Let us take your savings and start that business that sounds so foolish but, with two minds like ours, could really take off. Let us go down to the beach and watch the hurricane. Let us get married right now. Let us lose these boring friends of yours and go off somewhere by ourselves. Let us have sex in the elevator. Let us invest your money in this hot tip I just got. Let us laugh at the rules. Let us walk into this restaurant dressed in our T-shirts and jeans. Let us see how fast your car can go. Let us live a little.

Such is the flavor of sociopathic "spontaneity" and risk taking and "charm," and though we may chuckle about the obvious come-ons when we read them, the overall approach has met with noteworthy success time and again. Someone who is unfettered by conscience can easily make us feel that our lives are tediously rule-bound and lackluster, and that we should join him in what is typically represented as a more meaningful or exhilarating form of existence. Beginning with Eve and the serpent, our history books and our classic fiction are filled with tales of people who have been taken in and sometimes destroyed by the slick talk and magnetism of risk takers and evildoers—Dickie Greenleaf and the talented Mr. Ripley, Samson and Delilah, River City and Harold Hill, Trilby and Svengali, Norman Mailer and Jack Henry Abbott, Empress Alexandra and the seemingly immortal Rasputin. And from our own lives, we have memories of brushes with such people that send little cold chills up our spines. That is, if we are lucky we have had only brushes. The unfortunate must live with the indelible memories of outright personal catastrophes that occurred when they fell victim to the charm of the shameless.

Moreover, the shameless know us much better than we know them. We have an extremely hard time seeing that a person has no conscience, but a person who has no conscience can instantly recognize someone who is decent and trusting. Even as a child, Skip knew which boy he could talk into acquiring his fireworks for him. As an adult, he immediately perceived that Juliette could live with him for decades and never question his florid activities. Doreen Littlefield saw an easy mark in Ivy, the receptionist, and understood perfectly well that Jackie Rubenstein was a caring person who could be counted on to assume more than her fair share of responsibility.

When a sociopath identifies someone as a good game piece, she studies that person. She makes it her business to know how that person can be manipulated and used, and, to this end, just how her chosen pawn can be flattered and charmed. In addition, she knows how to promote a sense of familiarity or intimacy by claiming that she and her victim are similar in some way. Victims often recall statements that affected them even after the sociopath was gone, such as, "You know, I think you and I are a lot alike," or "It's so clear to me that you're my soul mate." In retrospect, these remarks can feel supremely demeaning. Outrageously untrue, they haunt the mind nonetheless.

Relatedly, people without conscience have an uncanny sense of who will be vulnerable to a sexual overture, and seduction is another very common sociopathic technique. For most people, a sexual liaison involves an emotional tie, even if only fleetingly, and such ties are used by the coldly remorseless to get what they want—allegiance, financial support, information, a sense of "winning," or perhaps just a temporary relationship that has the appearance of being normal. This is an easily recognized story, and another one that repeats itself often in our literature and history. But seldom do we recognize the degree of power it bestows on sociopaths, power over individuals, of course, and also over groups of people, and institutions. A sociopath who is hiding out in an organization can have his or her tracks hidden indefinitely by just one or two normal individuals who have made the single mistake of consummating their attraction to this charmingly dangerous person. Doreen, for example, was able to pose as a psychologist primarily because letters of reference were written by two people she had manipulated sexually. And when Jackie tried to expose Doreen's sociopathic behavior, a third person, the unit director, ran interference probably for the same reason, and the seductive "Dr." Littlefield remained at the hospital for six additional years.

And sexual seduction is only one aspect of the game. We are seduced as well by the acting skills of the sociopath. Since the scaffolding of a life without conscience is deception and illusion, intelligent sociopaths often become proficient at acting, and even at some of the particular techniques employed by professional actors. Paradoxically, the visible signs of emotion at will can become second nature to the cold-blooded—the appearance of intense interest in another person's problems or enthusiasms, chest-thumping patriotism, righteous indignation, blushing modesty, weepy sadness. Crocodile tears at will are a sociopathic trademark. Making sure that Ivy would see and be psychologically seduced by them, Doreen cried crocodile tears over her patient Dennis, and no doubt she cried them in front of Ivy again, profusely, when she inevitably made up the terrible, painful illness that "forced" her to have her little dog put to sleep.

Crocodile tears from the remorseless are especially likely when a conscience-bound person gets a little too close to confronting a sociopath with the truth. A sociopath who is about to be cornered by another person will turn suddenly into a piteous weeping figure whom no one, in good conscience, could continue to pressure. Or the opposite: Sometimes a cornered sociopath will adopt a posture of righteous indignation and anger in an attempt to scare off her accuser, as Doreen did with the hospital directors when she was finally fired.

Being natural actors, conscienceless people can make full use of social and professional roles, which constitute excellent ready-made masks that other people are loath to look behind. Roles help us organize our complex society, and they are tremendously important to us. If we see suspicious behavior, we may eventually question someone named Doreen Littlefield, but we are quite unlikely to question someone called *Dr.* Doreen Littlefield, no matter how unusual her behavior. We relate to the title of *doctor,* which holds a clear and positive meaning for us, and we do not think too hard about the human being who calls herself that. To some extent, the same is true for people who have (legally or illegally) assumed roles and titles in the arenas of leadership, business, organized religion, education, or parenthood. Seldom do the neighbors scrutinize the behavior of the church deacon or the town selectman or the high school principal or a business prodigy like Skip. We believe promises from such people because we assign to the individual the integrity of the role itself. In like fashion, we almost never challenge a neighbor's parenting practices, even when we fear that a child is being abused, and often our logic is no more substantial than "*He*'s the parent."

In addition, we are distracted from a person's actual behavior when he represents himself as in some way benevolent, creative, or insightful. We do not suspect people who claim to be animal lovers, for example. We give extra leeway to those who identify themselves as artists or intellectuals, in part because we attribute any departures from the norm to eccentricities we, as ordinary people, could not possibly understand. In general, our regard for such groups is a constructive sentiment, but it does sometimes open the door for sociopaths who can mimic the others.

Worse, our respect for people who appear to be inspired and benevolent leaders can be abused—has been abused many times—to cataclysmic ends. With a leader, especially one who claims to have a sublime mission, as with a doctor or a priest or a parent, we tend to bestow the qualities of the role on the individual, and to follow the individual accordingly. Benjamin Wolman, founder and editor of the *International Journal of Group Tensions*, writes, "Usually human cruelty increases when an aggressive sociopath gains an uncanny, almost hypnotic control over large numbers of people. History is full of chieftains, prophets, saviors, gurus, dictators, and other sociopathic megalomaniacs who managed to obtain support . . . and incited people to violence." Insidiously, when such a "savior" abducts the normal population to his purposes, he usually begins with an appeal to them as good people who would like to improve the condition of humanity, and then insists that they can achieve this by following his own aggressive plan.

In a confusing irony, conscience can be rendered partially blind because people without conscience use, as weapons against us, many of the fundamentally positive tools we need to hold society together—empathic emotions, sexual bonds, social and professional roles, regard for the compassionate and the creative, our desire to make the world a better place, and the organizing rule of authority. And people who do hideous things do not look like people who do hideous things. There is no "face of evil." If we could somehow subtract all its horrifying connotations, the actual face of Saddam Hussein looks rather avuncular, and has often been recorded as having a big friendly smile. Hitler's face, had it not become an icon of evil because of the atrocities his life engendered, might be considered almost comical, Chaplinesque as it were, in its foolish expression. Lizzy Borden looked like all the other laced-up Victorian ladies in Fall River, Massachusetts. Pamela Smart is pretty. Ted Bundy was so handsome that women sent marriage proposals to him on death row, and for every leering Charles Manson, there is the radiantly innocent countenance of a John Lee Malvo.

We try, consciously or tacitly, to judge a person's character by his or her appearance, but this book-by-its-cover strategy is ineffective in nearly all cases. In the real world, the bad guys do not look the way they are supposed to. They do not resemble werewolves or Hannibal

Lechter or Tony Perkins staring at a corpse in a rocking chair. On the contrary, they look like us.

Gaslight

Being targeted by a sociopath is a very frightening experience, even when that sociopath is not of the violent variety. In 1944, George Cukor directed a psychological thriller entitled *Gaslight,* in which a beautiful young woman, played by Ingrid Bergman, is made to feel she is going insane. Her fear that she is losing her mind is inflicted on her systematically by Charles Boyer, who plays her evil but charming new husband. Among a number of other dirty tricks, Boyer arranges for Bergman to hear sounds in the attic when he is absent, and for the gaslight to dim by itself, in a menacing house where her aunt was mysteriously murdered years before. Of course, no one believes Bergman about the noises in the attic or the gaslight or much of anything else, and her gradual descent into doubting her own reality has found its way into English idiom as "to be gaslighted." Boyer is not violent. He never strikes Bergman. Much more sinister—he causes her to lose faith in her own perceptions.

To suspect, and to try to explain to others that one has been targeted by a sociopath, is to be gaslighted. Jackie Rubenstein was a good example of this phenomenon when she confronted Doreen Littlefield with the cruelty she had done to Dennis. Afterward, Jackie phoned a friend for support because she felt she was losing her mind. And when she tried to relate her discovery about Doreen to the unit director, he politely but clearly echoed Doreen's implication that Jackie had gone a little crazy along with her paranoid patient.

When Jackie accused Doreen of a vicious act toward an unoffending patient, the natural question was, Why would a person like that do such a horrible thing? This is the question others always ask, overtly or by intimation, and it is such a bewildering, unanswerable question that the one who suspects the sociopath usually ends up asking it, too, only to find that she has no rational-sounding explanation. And like the innocent new bride in *Gaslight*, she may come to lose faith, partially or completely, in her own perceptions. Certainly she will hesitate to tell her story again, since trying to expose the sociopath casts doubts on her own credibility and maybe even on her sanity. These doubts, our own and other people's, are painful, and readily convince us to keep our mouths shut. Over the years, listening to hundreds of patients who have been targeted by sociopaths, I have learned that within an organization or a community, in the event that a sociopath is finally revealed to all and sundry, it is not unusual to find that several people suspected all along, each one independently, each one in silence. Each one felt gaslighted, and so each one kept her crazy-sounding secret to herself.

Why would a person like that do such a horrible thing? we ask ourselves. By "a person like that," we mean a normal-looking person, a person who looks just like us. We mean a person in a professional role, or an animal lover, or a parent or a spouse, or maybe a charming someone we have had dinner, or more, with. And by "such a horrible thing," we mean a negative act that is inexplicably bizarre, because there is no way, based on our own feelings and normal motivations, that we can explain why anyone would ever want to do it in the first place. Why would a smart, handsome, privileged boy like Skip want to slaughter small animals? In adulthood, why would fabulously successful Skip, married to the beautiful daughter of a billionaire, risk his reputation by breaking the arm of an employee? Why would Dr. Littlefield, a psychologist and the nicest person in the world, suddenly mount a brutal psychological attack on a recovering patient, and a VIP at that? Why would she, an established professional person, knowing she would be found out, make up a meaningless whole-cloth lie just to scare a young intern?

These are the kinds of questions we ask ourselves when we are exposed to sociopathic behavior, and in most cases, we cannot come up with answers that sound plausible to us. Speculate as we may, we cannot imagine *why*. Nothing sounds believable, so we think there must be a misunderstanding, or maybe we have greatly exaggerated something in our observations. We think this way because the conscience-bound mind is qualitatively different from the conscience-free mind, and what sociopaths want, what motivates them, is completely outside our experience. In order to harm a mentally ill person intentionally, as Doreen did, or to break someone's arm, as Skip did, most of us would have to be seriously threatened by the person we were hurting, or be under the influence of a compelling emotion such as rage. Performing such actions calmly, for fun, has no place in the emotional repertoire of normal people.

Sociopaths, people with no intervening sense of obligation based in attachments to others, typically devote their lives to interpersonal games, to "winning," to domination for the sake of domination. The rest of us, who do possess conscience, may be able to understand this motivational scheme conceptually, but when we see it in real life, its contours are so alien that we often fail to "see" it at all. Many people without conscience will behave self-destructively simply for the purposes of the game. Stamp Man spent half his life in jail for the thrill, every few years, of making a few postal workers and police officers scurry around for an hour or so. Doreen gleefully put her own career at significant risk just to damage her colleague's a little. These are behaviors we are not prepared to understand, or even believe. We will doubt our own sense of reality first.

And often our self-doubts are extreme. As an illustration, there was the remarkable public reaction, which continued for thirty years after her death, to a career criminal named Barbara Graham. In 1955, at the age of thirty-two, Graham was executed at San Quentin for her part in the especially brutal murder of an elderly widow named Mabel Monahan. Mrs. Monahan, like Ingrid Bergman's murdered aunt in *Gaslight*, had been rumored to keep a cache of jewels in her house. Graham and three accomplices entered the house, and when no jewels were forthcoming, Graham (nicknamed "Bloody Babs" by the media) pistol-whipped the elderly woman, nearly obliterating her face, and then suffocated her to death with a pillow.

Recorded at her execution, Bloody Babs's last words were, "Good people are always so sure they're right." This assertion was delivered calmly, almost with an air of sympathy, and as an effective gaslighting technique, it was a fairly good line. It caused many to doubt their own sense of reality concerning Graham, and refocused the public's attention on her role as an attractive mother of three young children, rather than on her grisly behavior. After her death, she became the subject of emotional debate, and even today, against the weight of considerable evidence, there are those who maintain that Graham was innocent. Out of the public's self-doubt sprang two films about her, both entitled *I Want to Live!* The first starred Susan Hayward, who won an Oscar for her performance, and a 1983 television remake featured Lindsay Wagner. In both versions, Graham, the sadistic murderess, was portrayed as a poignantly misunderstood woman who was framed.

Barbara Graham's last words—"Good people are always so sure they're right"—had a gaslighting effect precisely because the truth is quite the opposite. In fact, one of the more striking characteristics of good people is that they are almost never completely sure they are right. Good people question themselves constantly, reflexively, and subject their decisions and actions to the exacting scrutiny of an intervening sense of obligation rooted in their attachments to other people. The self-questioning of conscience seldom admits absolute certainty into the mind, and even when it does, certainty feels treacherous to us, as if it may trick us into punishing someone unjustly, or performing some other unconscionable act. Even legally, we speak of "beyond a reasonable doubt" rather than of complete certainty. In the end, Barbara Graham understood us far better than we understood her, and her parting remark pushed an irrational but very sensitive psychological button in the conscience-bound people who survived her—the fear that they had made a decision based on *too much certainty.*

Adding to our insecurity, most of us comprehend instinctively that there are shades of good and bad, rather than absolute categories. We know in our hearts there is no such thing as a person who is 100 percent good, and so we assume there must be no such thing as a person who is 100 percent bad. And perhaps philosophically—and certainly theologically—this is true. After all, in the Judeo-Christian tradition, the devil himself is a fallen angel. Probably there are no absolutely good human beings and no utterly bad ones. However—psychologically speaking, there definitely are people who possess an intervening sense of constraint based in emotional attachments, and other people who have no such sense. And to fail to understand this is to place people of conscience, and all the Mabel Monahans of the world, in danger.

How Do We Keep the Blinders Off?

My daughter's fifth-grade class had a field trip, and I was one of the chaperones. We went to see a play called *Freedom Train*, about Harriet Tubman and the Underground Railroad. On the noisy bus ride back to school, one of the boys was picking on another boy, poking him and pulling his hair. The quiet boy being poked was developmentally delayed, friendless, I am told, and did not have a clue how to defend himself. Even before one of the adults could intervene, a petite girl seated just behind the two boys tapped the tormentor on the shoulder and said, "That's really mean. Quit it."

The person who recognized this antisocial behavior and publicly objected to it was ten years old and all of four feet tall. The boy she had spoken to stuck his tongue out at her and leapt over to another bus seat to be with one of his pals. She watched him go and then calmly resumed the game of rock-paper-scissors she had been playing with the girl next to her.

What happens to us while we are growing up? Why do adults stop saying "Quit it" to the bullies? The grown-up bullies are more powerful, but then, so are we. Will this healthy little girl behave with the same kind of dignity and self-assurance when she is thirty years old and a foot and a half taller? Will she be another Harriet Tubman, albeit with a different cause? Sadly, given our present child-rearing practices, the odds are against it.

We raise our children, especially girls, to ignore their spontaneous reactions—we teach them not to rock the societal boat—and this is a good and necessary lesson when the spontaneous reaction involved would be to strike out violently with fists or words, or to steal an attractive item from a store, or to insult a stranger in a supermarket line. But another kind of spontaneous reaction, equally suppressed by our conflict-avoidant society, is the "Ick!" reaction, the natural sense of moral outrage. By the time she is thirty, the valiant little girl's "Ick!"—her tendency to respond, to rock the boat, when someone's actions are "really mean"—may have been excised from her behavior, and perhaps from her very mind.

In their book *Women's Anger: Clinical and Developmental Perspectives*, gender psychologists Deborah Cox, Sally Stabb, and Karin Bruckner document the ways girls and women perceive social responses to their outrage. Cox, Stabb, and Bruckner write that "the majority of interactions they [girls and women] describe involve rejection of either the anger, the girl or woman, or both. This takes the form of either direct attack through criticism or defensive response, or more passive rejection such as withdrawal and minimization of the girl's or woman's concerns and feelings." And based on her studies of adolescent girls, educator Lyn Mikel Brown maintains that idealized femininity can dangerously endorse "silence over outspokenness."

To keep the blinders off our life-enhancing seventh sense, as with most improvements in the human condition, we must start with our children. A part of healthy conscience is being able to confront consciencelessness. When you teach your daughter, explicitly or by passive rejection, that she must ignore her outrage, that she must be kind and accepting to the point of not defending herself or other people, that she must not rock the boat for any reason, you are not strengthening her prosocial sense; you are damaging it—and the first person she will stop protecting is herself. Cox, Stabb, and Bruckner argue emphatically that "the requirement to suppress outrage at the other robs the woman of an opportunity to develop this kind of autonomy." Instead, as Lyn Mikel Brown has said, we need to suggest "the possibility, even under the most oppressive conditions, for creative refusal and resistance."

Do not set her up to be gaslighted. When she observes that someone who is being really mean is being really mean, tell her she is right and that it is okay to say so out loud. Jackie Rubenstein chose to believe her patient Dennis, and not to believe her dangerous colleague Doreen Littlefield. It was a good, moral choice. She said, effectively, "That's really mean. Quit it," though saying so out loud caused her to be viewed as a troublemaker by many of the less insightful people around her.

As for the boys—in *Raising Cain: Protecting the Emotional Life of Boys*, leading child psychologists Dan Kindlon and Michael Thompson record their concern about the frequency with which "vulnerable fathers turn to time-honored defensive responses to maintain the fiction that 'father knows best.' " Parents, especially fathers, typically teach their sons to obey authority no matter what, and given the wrong cultural and political circumstances, circumstances that have occurred with morbid regularity throughout history, this is a lesson that may well come with a suicide clause. That parents wish to foster a certain respect for legitimate authority is understandable, and probably important for the functioning of society as we know it. But to drill children in reflexive, no-questions-asked obedience is to beat a horse that is more than half-dead already. Obedience to apparent authority is a knee-jerk reaction in most people quite without training, and to sensitize this reflex is to make our children hypervulnerable to any aggressive or sociopathic "authority" who may come along later in their lives.

To everyone's detriment, obedience and the higher values of patriotism and duty can become indistinguishable motivations. Enhanced in this way, reflexive obedience can consume the individual before he even has a chance to wonder whether he himself might be the best authority when it comes to his own life and his own country, and long before he can ask questions such as "Do I and my countrymen really want to fight and perhaps die for this external 'authority's' self-interest?"

Still, I believe we may now be standing at the edge of a modern possibility thousands of years in the making. In the past, for stark reasons of survival, human beings truly needed their children not to upset any hard-won applecarts, not to question things too much, not to disobey orders. Life was physically hard and precarious, and children who challenged our authority might all too easily end up as dead children. And so, until recent centuries, we raised humans for whom moral outrage was an extreme luxury, and to whom the questioning of authority felt life-threatening. In this way, generation after generation, we were unwittingly set up for sociopathic takeovers. But now, for most of us in the developed world, survival conditions no longer hold. We can stop. We can let our children question things. And when they are grown, they can, without doubting their own senses, look the grown-up bullies in the eye and say, "That's really mean. Quit it."

But what about those of us who are already grown, we who have had decades of practice in ignoring our own instincts? How can we avoid being gaslighted, and allow ourselves to recognize the people around us who have no conscience? This is the concern addressed in the next chapter. It is an interesting question with a rather surprising answer.

SIX

how to recognize the remorseless

In the desert, an old monk had once advised a traveler, the voices of God and the Devil are scarcely distinguishable.

—Loren Eiseley

In my practice, one of the questions I am asked most often is, "How can I tell whom to trust?" Since my patients are survivors of psychological trauma, most of whom have been devastated by other human beings, this is not a surprising concern for them to have. On the other hand, my feeling is that this issue is a pressing one for most of us, even those who have not endured severe trauma, and that we all try very hard to assess the level of conscience that exists, or not, in other people. We are especially interested in the conscience quotient of the people we have close relationships with, and when we meet an attractive new person, we often invest considerable mental energy in suspiciousness over, guesses about, and wishful thinking concerning this question.

The untrustworthy do not wear special shirts, or marks on their foreheads, and the fact that we must often make crucial decisions about other people based on not much more than guesswork leads us to irrational strategies that readily become lifelong superstitions.

"Don't trust anyone over thirty," "Never trust a man," "Never trust a woman," "Never trust anyone" are the most popular examples. We want a clear rule, even a sweeping one, because knowing whom to be wary of is so important to us, but these wide-brush strategies are ineffective, and, worse, they tend to produce anxiety and unhappiness in our lives.

Apart from knowing someone well for many years, there is no foolproof decision rule or litmus test for trustworthiness, and it is extremely important to acknowledge this fact, unnerving though it may be. Uncertainty in this regard is simply a part of the human condition, and I have never known anyone who got around it completely, except by the most extraordinary luck. Furthermore, to imagine there is an effective method—a method that one has thus far been unable to figure out—is to beat up on oneself in a way that is demeaning and unfair.

When it comes to trusting other people, we all make mistakes. Some of these mistakes are larger than others.

Having said this, when people ask me about trust, I reply that there is bad news and good news. The bad news is that there truly are individuals who have no conscience, and these individuals are not to be trusted at all. Perhaps an average of four people in a random group of one hundred are limited in this way. The good news—the very good news—is that at least ninety-six people out of a hundred are bound by the constraints of conscience, and can therefore be counted on to behave according to a reasonably high baseline of decency and responsibility—to behave, in other words, more or less as well as you and I do. And to my mind, this second fact is a great deal more compelling than the first. It means, astonishingly, that to a certain standard of prosocial behavior, our interpersonal world should be about ninety-six percent safe.

And so why does the world seem to be so terribly unsafe? How do we explain the six o'clock news, or even our own personal bad experiences? What is going on here? Could it conceivably be that a mere 4 percent of the population is responsible for nearly all of the human disasters that occur in the world, and in our individual lives? This is an arresting question, one that offers to overhaul many of our assumptions about human society. So I will repeat that the phenomenon of conscience is overwhelmingly powerful, persistent, and prosocial. Unless under the spell of a psychotic delusion, extreme rage, inescapable deprivation, drugs, or a destructive authority figure, a person who is conscience-bound does not—in some sense he *cannot*—kill or rape in cold blood, torture another person, steal someone's life savings, trick someone into a loveless relationship as sport, or willfully abandon his own child.

Could you?

When we see people doing such things, either in the news or in our own lives, who are they? On the rare occasion, they are formally insane, or under the pressure of some radical emotion. Sometimes they are members of a group that is desperately deprived, or they are substance abusers, or the followers of a malevolent leader. But most often they are none of these. Rather, most often, they are people who have no conscience. They are sociopaths.

Certainly the very worst of the unthinkable deeds we read about in our newspapers and tacitly ascribe to "human nature"—though the events shock us as normal human beings—are not reflective of normal human nature at all, and we insult and demoralize ourselves when we assume so. Mainstream human nature, though far from perfect, is very much governed by a disciplining sense of interconnectedness, and the genuine horrors we see on television, and sometimes endure in our personal lives, do not reflect typical humankind. Instead, they are made possible by something quite alien to our nature—the cold and complete absence of conscience.

This is, I think, somewhat difficult for many people to accept. We have a hard time acknowledging that particular individuals are shameless by their nature, and the rest of us not so, due in part to what I refer to as the "shadow theory" of human nature. Shadow theory—the simple and probably accurate notion that we all have a "shadow side" not necessarily apparent from our usual behavior—maintains in its most extreme form that anything doable or feelable by one human being is potentially doable or feelable by all. In other words, under certain circumstances (though they are circumstances we are hard-pressed to imagine) anyone at all could be, for example, a death-camp commandant. Ironically, good and kindhearted people are often the most willing to subscribe to this theory in the radical form that proposes they could, in some bizarre situation, be mass murderers. It feels more democratic and less condemnatory (and somehow less alarming) to believe that everyone is a little shady than to accept that a few human beings live in a permanent and absolute moral nighttime. To admit that some people literally have no conscience is not technically the same as saying that some human beings are evil, but it is disturbingly close. And good people want very much not to believe in the personification of evil.

Of course, though not everyone could be a death-camp commandant, many if not most people are capable of overlooking the horrific activities of such a person, owing to the viscosity of psychological denial, moral exclusion, and blind obedience to authority. Asked about our sense that we are not safe in our own world, Albert Einstein once said, "The world is a dangerous place to live, not because of the people who are evil, but because of the people who don't do anything about it."

To do something about shameless people, we must first identify them. So, in our individual lives, how do we recognize the one person out of (more or less) twenty-five who has no conscience and who is potentially dangerous to our resources and our well-being? Deciding whether or not someone is trustworthy usually requires knowing that person well for a long time, and in the case of identifying a sociopath, much better and longer than one would have allowed had the sociopath been wearing a mark on his forehead at the outset. This harrowing dilemma is simply a part of the human condition. But even given the familiarity requirement, the pressing question remains, "How can I tell whom to trust?"—or more to the point, whom *not* to trust.

After listening for almost twenty-five years to the stories my patients tell me about sociopaths who have invaded and injured their lives, when I am asked, "How can I tell whom not to trust?" the answer I give usually surprises people. The natural expectation is that I will describe some sinister-sounding detail of behavior or snippet of body language or threatening use of language that is the subtle giveaway. Instead, I take people aback by assuring them that the tip-off is none of these things, for none of these things is reliably present. Rather, the best clue is, of all things, the pity play. The most reliable sign, the most universal behavior of unscrupulous people is not directed, as one might imagine, at our fearfulness. It is, perversely, an appeal to our sympathy.

I first learned this when I was still a graduate student in psychology and had the opportunity to interview a court-referred patient the system had already identified as a "psychopath." He was not violent, preferring instead to swindle people out of their money with elaborate investment scams. Intrigued by this individual and what could possibly motivate him—I was young enough to think he was a rare sort of person—I asked, "What is important to you in your life? What do you want more than anything else?" I thought he might say "getting money," or "staying out of jail," which were the activities to which he devoted most of his time. Instead, without a moment's hesitation, he replied, "Oh, that's easy. What I like better than anything else is when people feel sorry for me. The thing I really want more than anything else out of life is people's pity."

I was astonished, and more than a little put off. I think I would have liked him better if he had said "staying out of jail," or even "getting money." Also, I was mystified. Why would this man—why would anyone—wish to be pitied, let alone wish to be pitied above all other ambitions? I could not imagine. But now, after twenty-five years of listening to victims, I realize there is an excellent reason for the sociopathic fondness for pity. As obvious as the nose on one's face, and just as difficult to see without the help of a mirror, the explanation is that good people will let pathetic individuals get by with murder, so to speak, and therefore any sociopath wishing to continue with his game, whatever it happens to be, should play repeatedly for none other than pity.

More than admiration—more even than fear—pity from good people is carte blanche. When we pity, we are, at least for the moment, defenseless, and like so many of the other essentially positive human characteristics that bind us together in groups—social and professional roles, sexual bonds, regard for the compassionate and the creative, respect for our leaders—our emotional vulnerability when we pity is used against us by those who have no conscience. Most of us would agree that giving special dispensation to someone who is incapable of feeling guilt is a bad idea, but often, when an individual presents himself as pathetic, we do so nonetheless.

Pity and sympathy are forces for good when they are reactions to deserving people who have fallen on misfortune. But when these sentiments are wrested out of us by the undeserving, by people whose behavior is consistently antisocial, this is a sure sign that something is wrong, a potentially useful danger signal that we often overlook. Perhaps the most easily recognized example is the battered wife whose sociopathic husband beats her routinely and then sits at the kitchen table, head in his hands, moaning that he cannot control himself and that he is a poor wretch whom she must find it in her heart to forgive. There are countless other examples, a seemingly endless variety, some even more flagrant than the violent spouse and some almost subliminal. And for those of us who do have conscience, such situations, no matter how brazen, seem to present us emotionally with a kind of embedded figure puzzle, in which the background design (the appeal for pity) continually overcomes our perceptions of the more important embedded picture (the antisocial behavior).

In long retrospect, sociopathic appeals for pity are preposterous and chilling. Skip implied that he deserved sympathy because he had broken someone's arm. Doreen Littlefield represented herself as a poor overworked soul who was too sensitive to witness her patients' pain. From prison, a lovely and endearing Barbara Graham explained to reporters that society was preventing her from taking proper care of her children. And as for the likes of the aforementioned death-camp official—in the 1945 interrogations that preceded the Nuremberg War Crimes Tribunal, testimony from actual death-camp guards included their descriptions of how awful it was to be in charge of the crematoriums, on account of the smell. In interviews highlighted by British historian Richard Overy, the guards complained that it was difficult for them to eat their sandwiches at work.

Sociopaths have no regard whatsoever for the social contract, but they do know how to use it to their advantage. And all in all, I am sure that if the devil existed, he would want us to feel very sorry for him.

When deciding whom to trust, bear in mind that the combination of consistently bad or egregiously inadequate behavior with frequent plays for your pity is as close to a warning mark on a conscienceless person's forehead as you will ever be given. A person whose behavior includes both of these features is not necessarily a mass murderer, or even violent at all, but is still probably not someone you should closely befriend, take on as your business partner, ask to take care of your children, or marry.

Poor Luke

What about the most precious component of the social contract? What about love? Here is one woman's quiet calamity, a story that will never be on the six o'clock news.

My patient Sydney was not pretty. At forty-five, she had dirty blond hair that was turning gray and a round motherly body that had never been glamorous. But she owned a fine intellect and a long list of academic and professional accomplishments. At a university in her home state of Florida, she had been promoted to an associate professorship in epidemiology before she was thirty. She studied the population effects of substances used in indigenous medicines, and before her marriage she had traveled extensively in Malaysia, South America, and the Caribbean. When she moved from Florida to Massachusetts, she became a consultant to an ethnopharmacology group based in Cambridge. But I liked her most for her gentle demeanor and the thoughtful, introspective approach she took to her life. One of the things I remember best about her was the soft warmth of her speaking voice during the brief fifteen therapy sessions we had together.

Sydney was divorced from a man named Luke. The divorce had drained her life savings and caused her to go into debt, because she had needed to make sure she got custody of her son, Jonathan, who was eight when I knew Sydney, and only five at the time of the divorce. Luke had put up an expensive struggle, not because he loved Jonathan, but because he was enraged with Sydney for making him move out of her house.

The house in South Florida had a swimming pool. Luke loved the pool.

"Luke was living in this shabby little apartment when I met him," Sydney told me. "That should've raised a red flag for me right there, a thirty-five-year-old man who'd gone to graduate school at NYU—city planning, actually—living in that awful little place. But I ignored it. He said he really liked the big pool his apartment complex had. So when he saw I had my own pool, he got all happy. What can I tell you? My husband married me for my pool. Well, that's not entirely true, but in retrospect, it was definitely part of it."

Sydney overlooked Luke's lifestyle, and his attraction to hers, because she thought she had found something rare, an extremely intelligent, attractive thirty-five-year-old man, with no wife and no ex-wives, whose interests seemed similar to hers, and who treated her well.

"He treated me very well at first, I must say. He took me out. He always brought me flowers. I remember all those birds-of-paradise in long boxes, all those orange flowers. I had to go out and buy some really tall vases. I don't know. He was soft-spoken and sort of quietly charming—we had great conversations. He was another academic type, like me, or so I thought. When I met him, he was working on a planning project through a friend of his at the university. Always dressed up in suits. Actually, that's where I met him, the university. Nice, upstanding place to meet somebody, wouldn't you say? He told me he thought we were a lot alike, and I guess I believed him."

As the weeks passed, Sydney learned that since Luke had been twenty or so, he had lived with a succession of women, always in their homes, and that having a place of his own, even an inexpensive one, had been an unusual departure from his preferred situation. But she overlooked this information also, because she was falling in love with Luke. And she thought he was in love with her, too, because that was what he told her.

"I'm just a frumpy academic. No one had ever been so romantic with me. It was a good time—I should probably confess that. Too bad it had to be so short. Anyway . . . There I was, this frumpy thirty-five-year-old career type, and all of a sudden I was thinking about a white wedding, the whole nine yards. I'd never done that before. I mean, I always thought it was a silly fairy tale they tell little girls, not something I'd ever have—or want—and there I was, wanting it, *planning* it even.

"As for the fact that he'd lived off those other women—do you believe I actually felt sorry for him? I thought he was searching for the right person or something, and they usually just threw him out after a while. Now I understand why, but I certainly didn't then. I thought, How lonely, how sad. He said one of those women was actually killed in a car crash. He cried about it when he told me that. I felt so bad for him."

Six weeks after they met, Luke moved into Sydney's house, and eight months later they were married, a big church wedding, followed by a formal dinner reception paid for by her family.

"Doesn't the bride's family always pay for the wedding?" she asked me wryly.

Two months after the wedding, Sydney discovered she was pregnant. She had always wanted children, but had believed she would never marry. Now her dream of motherhood was coming true, and she was overjoyed.

"It seemed like such a miracle to me, especially when the baby started to move. I kept saying to myself, There's a brand-new person in there, someone who never was before, someone I'm going to love for the rest of my life. It was incredible. Luke was obviously a lot less excited than me, but still he said he wanted the baby, too. He said he was just nervous. He thought I was ugly while I was pregnant, but I figured he was just being more honest than most men are about it. Ironic, huh?

"I was so happy about the baby that I didn't let myself know what I think I already knew, if that makes any sense. I think I realized the marriage wasn't going to work while I was pregnant. The doctor told me the worst risk of miscarriage was over after the first three months, and so of course I took this literally, and at the fourth month, I went out and bought a crib. I remember it was on the day they delivered it, Luke came home and told me he'd quit his job. Just like that. It was as if he knew that now he had me. I was about to have a baby, and so I would definitely take care of things. I would take care of him financially because now I didn't have a choice. He was wrong about that, but I can see why he thought it. He must've thought I'd do just about anything to hold on to that semblance of family."

Of course, that was not what Luke said to Sydney, or to her friends or her family. He told them all that he was depressed, far too depressed to work, and whenever others were around, he fell silent, looked hangdog, and in general played the part of a depressed person. To make matters even more confusing for Sydney, a number of people told her that depression among first-time fathers was common.

"But I never really thought he was depressed," Sydney told me. "Something didn't seem right. I've been a little depressed myself at times, and this just wasn't it. For one thing, he had way too much energy when there was something he really wanted to do. And also—this seems like a small thing, but it made me pretty nuts—he wouldn't get help. I said we should spend some money for a therapist, or maybe some kind of medication. But he avoided that idea like the plague."

When Jonathan was born, Sydney took a two-month maternity leave from her teaching, which meant that all three members of the family were at home together, since Luke was not working. But Luke seldom even looked at his new son, preferring to read magazines by the pool or to go out with his friends. And when Jonathan cried, as newborns will, Luke would get angry, sometimes enraged, and demand that Sydney do something about the noise.

"He acted like a martyr, I think is the best way to put it. He'd hold his ears and make these tormented faces and pace around, as if the baby were crying just specifically to create problems for *him*. I think I was supposed to feel sorry for him or something. It was creepy. I'd had a C-section, and I really could've used some help at first, but I ended up wishing that Jonathan and I could just be alone."

The same people who had told Sydney about depressed first-time fathers now assured her that new dads sometimes felt uncomfortable around their newborns and so kept their distance for a while. They insisted that Luke needed sympathy and patience.

"But Luke wasn't 'keeping his distance' the way they thought. He was totally oblivious. Jonathan might as well have been a bundle of rags, for all he cared—an annoying little bundle of rags. Still, don't you know, I wanted to believe those people. I wanted to believe that somehow, *somehow,* if I could manage enough understanding and patience, everything was going to be okay. We were going to be a real family, eventually—I wanted so much to believe that."

When her maternity leave was over, Sydney went back to work and Luke stayed by the pool. Sydney contacted an au pair agency to find daytime child care, because it was clear that Luke was not going to take care of Jonathan. After a few weeks, the young sitter confided in Sydney that she felt "weird" keeping the baby with the father always present but never showing any interest.

"I can't understand why he never even looks at his baby. Is he quite all right, ma'am?" the sitter cautiously asked Sydney.

Using a variant of the excuse Luke had provided, an embarrassed Sydney told her, "He's going through a hard time in his life right now. You can just kind of pretend he's not there and you'll be fine."

Sydney recounted how the sitter looked out through the glass doors of the den toward the swimming pool, presumably seeing a relaxed and tan Luke sitting there in the Florida late afternoon. Cocking her head to one side in curiosity, she said softly, "Poor man."

Sydney told me, "I'll always remember that. 'Poor man.' Poor Luke. It was how I felt about him, too, sometimes, despite myself."

But the truth was that the person Sydney had married was not "poor Luke" at all, nor was he a depressed first-time father, nor was he going through a hard time in his life. Rather, he was sociopathic. Luke had no intervening sense of obligation to other people, and his behavior, though not physically violent, reflected this dangerous fact.

For Luke, societal rules and interpersonal exp
to serve his advantage. He told Sydney that he lo
went so far as to marry her, primarily for the opportunit
himself as a kept man in her honestly earned and comfor
He used his wife's dearest and most private dreams to manip
her, and their son was an aggravation he moodily tolerated only be-
cause the baby seemed to seal her acceptance of his presence. Otherwise, he ignored his own child.

Soon he began to ignore Sydney as well.

"It was kind of like having a boarder, a boarder you don't like very much and who doesn't pay rent. He was just kind of there. For the most part, we lived these parallel lives. There was Jonathan and me, always together, and then there was Luke. I really don't know what he did most of the time. Sometimes he'd leave for a day or two. I don't know where he went—I stopped caring about it. Or sometimes he'd have a friend over for drinks, always unannounced, which could be kind of a problem at times. And he'd rack up big phone bills. But mostly he just sat around by the pool, or when the weather was bad, he'd come in and watch TV, or play computer games. You know, those computer games thirteen-year-old boys play.

"Oh, and I nearly forgot—for a couple of months, he collected lithographs. I don't know what put him onto that, but he was really excited about it for a while. He'd buy a new one—they were expensive, let me tell you—and he'd come bringing it in to show me, like a kid, like nothing was wrong between us and he wanted me to see the new addition to his art collection. He must've collected about thirty of them—never framed them—and then one day he just dropped the whole business. No more interest in lithographs. Over."

Sociopaths sometimes exhibit brief, intense enthusiasms—hobbies, projects, involvements with people—that are without commitment or follow-up. These interests appear to begin abruptly and for no reason, and to end the same way.

"I had a new husband and a new baby. It should've been one of

was one of the worst. I'd come
...e sitter would let me know that
...onathan all day, and after a while
...me so much that I couldn't even
...med to tell you this, but I slept in my
...

...est difficulty Sydney had in telling me her story
...embarrassment about what had happened to her life.
...it, "You can't imagine how humiliating it is to admit, even just to admit to yourself, that you actually married somebody like that. And I wasn't a kid when I did it, either. I was thirty-five already, not to mention I'd been around the world several times. I should've known better. But I just didn't see it. I didn't see it at all, and, to give myself a little break, I don't think anyone else who was around at the time saw it, either. These days, everybody tells me they never dreamed he'd end up acting that way. And everybody has a different theory about 'what's wrong with Luke.' If it weren't so embarrassing, it would be funny. Different friends have decided it's everything from schizophrenia to something like attention deficit disorder. Can you imagine?"

Unsurprisingly, not a single person guessed that Luke simply had no conscience and that this was why he ignored his obligations to his wife and his child. Luke's pattern did not fit anyone's images of sociopathy, even nonviolent sociopathy, because Luke, though he had a high IQ, was essentially passive. He did not go about cutting throats, either literally or figuratively, in an attempt to achieve power or wealth. He was no corporate shark, and certainly no fast-talking, high-octane Skip. He did not have enough vitality even to be an ordinary con man, or enough physical courage to rob banks (or post offices). He was not a mover. He was, in effect, a nonmover. His predominant ambition was to be inert, to avoid work, and to have someone else provide a comfortable lifestyle, and he exerted himself just enough to reach this middling goal.

And so how did Sydney finally recognize his remorselessness? It was the pity play.

"Even after that really ugly divorce, he still hung around the house, and I do mean nearly every day. He got another crummy little apartment, and he always slept there, but during the day he'd hang out at my house. I know now that I shouldn't have let him, but I felt sorry for him, and also he was paying a little more attention to Jonathan. When he'd come home from kindergarten, sometimes Luke would even meet him at the bus, walk him home, give him a little swimming lesson or something. I felt nothing for the man. I really never wanted to see him again, but I wasn't going out with anyone—like I'm going to trust another man, right?—and I thought it was a good thing if Jonathan could get to know his father, get a little attention from him. I figured it was worth the nuisance if my child could have at least part of a dad.

"Well, that was a mistake. My sister was the one who called the shot. She said, 'Luke doesn't have a relationship with Jonathan. He has a relationship with your house.' And oh boy, was she ever right. But then I couldn't get rid of him. Things got really awful and complicated and . . . creepy. It was really *creepy*."

She shuddered, then took a deep breath and went on.

"When he—Jonathan—was in the first grade, I realized I had to get Luke out of our lives once and for all. There was just no peace, no . . . well, I want to say joy. When someone doesn't care about you at all like that, having him around you so much really sucks out the peace and the joy from your life. He kept just showing up. He'd come in, or go out to the pool and make himself comfortable, just like he still lived there, and I'd get really morose, really tense. I'd stay in the house with the shades drawn just so he wouldn't be in my line of sight. It was crazy. Then I realized—Jonathan's spirits were going down, too. He didn't really want Luke around, either.

"So I started asking him to leave. Now, if I were over at somebody else's house and they asked me to leave, I'd leave—wouldn't you?—if only for my own dignity. Not Luke. He acted like he hadn't even heard me, which was fairly creepy all by itself, or he'd leave for a while, and then he'd come back just like nothing had happened. So I'd get really angry, and instead of just asking him to leave, I'd scream at him to get out, or I'd threaten to call the police. And do you know what he did?"

"He used Jonathan," I said.

"That's right. How did you know? He used Jonathan. For example, we were out by the pool, all three of us, and Luke started to cry. Actual *tears* came out of the man's eyes. Then I remember he picked up the net we used to skim the pool and started skimming, like he was a suffering martyr who only wanted to help, and then Jon got tearful, too, and he said—and I'll remember this for the rest of my life—Jonathan said, 'Oh no. Poor Daddy. Do we have to make him leave?'

"And then Luke looked at me, looked me right in the eyes, and it was as if I'd never met him before in my life. He looked that different. Those were the creepiest eyes I've ever seen, like beams of ice—it's really hard to explain. And I realized, all of a sudden, that in Luke's mind this was all some kind of a control game. It was some kind of a game, and I had lost, big-time. I was stunned."

Within a year after this scene by the pool, Sydney left Florida and her university position there and moved with Jonathan to the Boston area to be closer to her sister, and fifteen hundred miles away from Luke. A few months later, she started a brief therapy with me. She needed to work through some of the issues left over from her marriage, especially her self-blame that she had married Luke in the first place. She was an extremely resilient person, and I have every reason to think her life is happier now. She would sometimes joke that, in the case of her problem with Luke, the famous "geographic cure" just might work, although she knew that the longer journey of self-forgiveness would be more complicated.

Sydney was able to gain a certain understanding of her ex-husband's lack of conscience, and this new perspective was helpful to her. Her greatest remaining concern was the emotional vulnerability of her eight-year-old son, Jonathan. The last time I saw Sydney, she told me that she and Jonathan were still having tearful discussions about Florida and how much he felt sorry for Daddy.

SEVEN

the etiology of guiltlessness: what causes sociopathy?

Since adolescence I have wondered why so many people take pleasure in humiliating others. Clearly the fact that some are sensitive to the suffering of others proves that the destructive urge to hurt is not a universal aspect of human nature.

—*Alice Miller*

In many ways, Luke, Doreen, and Skip are very different from one another. Luke favors inertia. He likes to lounge, and to let responsible "friends" and family members take care of everything else. Doreen is envious, and a chronic malcontent. She exerts a great deal of energy trying to make other people look smaller so that she can feel bigger. And Skip would like to run the world, for his own benefit, of course, and as a grandiose form of entertainment. But what these three diversely motivated human beings have in common is that, in the interest of their individual ambitions, *they can do anything at all* without the slenderest glimmer of guilt. Each of them desires something different, but they all get what they want in exactly the same fashion, which is to say, completely without shame. Skip breaks the law and ruins careers and lives, and he feels nothing. Doreen makes her whole life into a lie, and torments the helpless for the thrill of making her colleagues look bad, and all without the slightest blip of embarrassment or accountability. For someone to take care of him, a rent-free house, and a swimming pool, Luke lovelessly marries a decent woman who wants to have a family, and then steals some of the joy from his son's childhood in an attempt to retain his own childlike dependency. And he makes such decisions without thinking twice, let alone being assailed by guilt.

None of these people has an intervening seventh sense of obligation based in emotional attachments. While, sadly, this commonality among them does not make them extremely rare, it does make them profoundly different from all people who do have conscience. All three are members of a group apart, a human category in which the distinguishing feature—the absence of conscience—cuts across all other personality features and even gender in terms of how individuals perceive their surroundings and go about their lives. Doreen is more like Luke and Skip than she is like any woman in the world who has conscience, and laconic Luke and driven Skip are more like each other than any conscience-bound man or woman of any temperament whatsoever.

What carves this deep and yet strangely invisible dividing line across the human race? Why do some people not have a conscience? What causes sociopathy?

Like so many human characteristics, both physical and psychological, the primary question is that of nature versus nurture. Is the characteristic born in the blood, or is it created by the environment? For most complex psychological features, the answer is, very probably, both. In other words, a predisposition for the characteristic is present at conception, but the environment regulates how it is expressed. This is true both for traits we consider negative and for those we think of as positive. For example, level of intelligence would appear to be strongly determined by genetic makeup but partly shaped by an elaborate toolbox of environmental factors as well, such as prenatal care, early stimulation, nutrition, and even birth order. Sociopathic deviance, a decidedly more negative characteristic, is probably no exception to this some-of-each paradigm. Research indicates that both nature and nurture are involved.

Psychologists have long known that many aspects of personality, such as extraversion and neuroticism, are influenced to some degree by genetic factors. Much of the scientific evidence for this is provided by studies comparing monozygotic (identical) and dizygotic (fraternal) twins. The underlying premise in such research is that identical twins share an environment and all of their genes, whereas fraternal twins share an environment but only about half of their genes. For any given trait, scientists assume that if the correlation (or likeness) for genetically identical twins is significantly greater than the correlation for genetically dissimilar twins, there is at least some genetic influence for that trait.

Researchers use a number that is double the difference between the identical twin correlation and the fraternal twin correlation to indicate the amount of variation thought to be accounted for by genetic factors. This number is referred to as the trait's "heritability," and studies on twins have shown that personality features determined by questionnaires (such as extraversion, neuroticism, authoritarianism, empathy, and so forth) have a heritability of between 35 and 50 percent. In other words, twin studies indicate that most measurable aspects of our personalities are 35 to 50 percent innate.

Heritability studies contain important information about sociopathy. A number of such studies have included the "Psychopathic Deviate" (Pd) scale of the *Minnesota Multiphasic Personality Inventory* (the *MMPI*). The Pd scale of the *MMPI* consists of multiple-choice questions that have been statistically formulated to sort out people with sociopathic personality traits from other groups of people. The inventory includes several validity measures as well, including a "Lie Scale" to expose attempts to beat the test. Overall in these studies, identical twins are twice or more as likely to have similar scores on the Pd scale as are fraternal twins, strongly suggesting at least some genetic role in the "Psychopathic Deviate" pattern.

In 1995, a major longitudinal study was published that investigated sociopathic traits and their absence in 3,226 pairs of male twins located through a register of people who had served in the United States armed services during the Vietnam War. By the same mathematical model, eight sociopathic symptoms and their absence were found to be significantly heritable. They are, in descending order of theoretical heritability: "fails to conform to social norms," "aggressive," "reckless," "impulsive," "fails to honor financial obligations," "inconsistent work," "never monogamous," and "lacks remorse." Still other studies have found that sociopaths have low "agreeableness," low "conscientiousness," and low "harm avoidance," all of which personality dimensions have a genetic component.

The Texas Adoption Project, which has now been in progress for over thirty years, is a highly regarded longitudinal study of more than five hundred adopted children. The study looks at the acquisition of intelligence and various personality features, including the "Psychopathic Deviate" pattern, by comparing adopted children, now grown, with both their biological and adoptive parents. The Texas Adoption Project reports that, where scores on the Pd scale are concerned, individuals resemble their birth mothers, whom they have never met, significantly more than they do the adoptive parents who raised them. From this research, a heritability estimate of 54 percent can be derived, and interestingly, this "Psychopathic Deviate" figure is consistent with the heritability estimates—35 to 50 percent—generally found in studies of other, more neutral personality characteristics (extraversion, empathy, and so forth).

Over and again, heritability studies come up with a statistical finding that has emotionally charged social and political implications—that indeed a person's tendency to possess certain sociopathic characteristics is partially born in the blood, perhaps as much as 50 percent so. To bring home the provocative nature of this research—it would indicate, for example, that before they were even born, at the very moment of conception, people such as Doreen, Luke, and Skip were already somewhat predisposed to become deceitful, reckless, faithless, and remorseless. When we make heritability statements about athletic ability or introversion, or even bipolar disorders or schizophrenia, somehow the information does not seem so shocking. But to say so about antisocial tendencies feels especially grim, though the same statistical approaches are used.

It is important to point out that such extremely complex characteristics are unlikely to be determined by a single gene, but are almost certainly oligogenic, meaning caused by multiple genes acting together. And the exact way in which these genes go about shaping brain function and then behavior is currently unknown. Getting from a person's DNA to a many-layered behavioral concept such as "fails to honor financial obligations" is a long, labyrinthine biochemical, neurological, and psychological trip, and is correspondingly daunting to study.

But research has already provided us with a few pointed hints. One important link in the neurobiological-behavioral segment of the chain may consist of altered functioning in the cerebral cortex of the sociopath. Some of the most interesting information about cortical functioning in sociopathy comes to us through studies of how human beings process language. As it turns out, even at the level of electrical activity in the brain, normal people react to emotional words (such as *love, hate, cozy, pain, happy, mother*) more rapidly and more intensely than to relatively neutral words (*table, chair, fifteen, later,* etc.) If I am given the task of deciding between words and nonwords, I will recognize *terror* over *lister* much faster, in terms of microseconds, than I will choose between *window* and *endock,* and my enhanced reaction to the emotional word *terror* can be measured by recording a tiny electrical reaction, called an "evoked potential," in my cerebral cortex. Such studies indicate that the brains of normal people attend to, remember, and recognize words that refer to emotional experiences preferentially to emotion-neutral words. *Love* will be recognized as a word faster than *look* will be, and a greater evoked potential will result in the brain, very much as if *love* were a more primal and meaningful piece of information than *look*.

Not so for sociopathic subjects who have been tested using language-processing tasks. In terms of reaction time and evoked potentials in the cortex, sociopathic subjects in these experiments respond to emotionally charged words no differently from neutral words. In sociopaths, the evoked potential for *sob* or *kiss* is no larger than the one for *sat* or *list*, very much as if emotional words were no more meaningful, or deeply coded by their brains, than any other words.

In related research using single-photon emission-computed tomography (brain-imaging technology), sociopathic subjects showed increased blood flow to the temporal lobes, relative to other subjects, when they were given a decision task that involved emotional words. To enable our concentration, you or I might exhibit such an increased cerebral blood flow if we were asked to solve a mildly challenging intellectual problem. In other words, sociopaths trying to complete an assignment based on emotional words, a task that would be almost neurologically instantaneous for normal people, reacted physiologically more or less as if they had been asked to work out an algebra problem.

Taken together, such studies indicate that sociopathy involves an altered processing of emotional stimuli at the level of the cerebral cortex. Why this altered processing occurs is not yet known, but it is likely to be the result of a heritable neurodevelopmental difference that can be either slightly compensated for, or made much worse, by child-rearing or cultural factors. This neurodevelopmental distinction is at least partially responsible for the still-unfathomed psychological difference between sociopaths and all other people, and its implications are startling. Sociopathy is more than just the absence of conscience, which alone would be tragic enough. Sociopathy is the inability to process emotional experience, including love and caring, except when such experience can be calculated as a coldly intellectual task.

Just as conscience is not merely the presence of guilt and remorse, but is based in our capacity to experience emotion and the attachments that result from our feelings, sociopathy is not just the absence of guilt and remorse. Sociopathy is an aberration in the ability to have and to appreciate real (noncalculated) emotional experience, and therefore to connect with other people within real (noncalculated) relationships. To state the situation concisely, and maybe a little too clearly for comfort: Not to have a moral sense flags an even more profound condition, as does the possession of conscience, because conscience never exists without the ability to love, and sociopathy is ultimately based in lovelessness.

A sociopath is someone who "fails to conform to social norms," or who is "never monogamous," or who "fails to honor financial obligations," for the straightforward reason that an obligation of any kind is something one feels toward beings, or toward a group of beings, who matter emotionally. And to a sociopath, we simply do not matter.

Sociopathy is, at its very essence, ice-cold, like a dispassionate game of chess. In this way, it is different from ordinary duplicitousness, narcissism, and even violence, which are often full of emotional heat. If necessary, most of us would lie to save the life of someone in our family, and it is something of a cliché to point out that a violent gang member (as opposed, perhaps, to his sociopathic leader) may conceivably feel loyalty and warmth toward the members of his gang, and tenderness for his mother and siblings. But Skip, even as a child, was not concerned with anyone, Dr. Littlefield could not care about her patients, and Luke could not love even his wife or his own child. In the workings of such minds, other people, even "friends" and family members, are serviceable game pieces at most.

Love is not a possibility, or even something that can be comprehended when another person shows it.

The only emotions that sociopaths seem to feel genuinely are the so-called "primitive" affective reactions that result from immediate physical pain and pleasure, or from short-term frustrations and successes. Frustration may engender anger or rage in a sociopath. And predatory success, winning at a game of cat and mouse (for example, Doreen's success in sending Jenna on a fool's errand across the muck of a hospital lawn), typically sparks aggressive affect and arousal, a "rush" that may be experienced as a moment of glee. These emotional reactions are seldom long-lasting, and they are referred to as neurologically "primitive" because, like all emotions, they originate in the evolutionally ancient limbic system of the brain, but, unlike the "higher" emotions, they are not significantly modified by the functions of the cerebral cortex.

As a counterpoint to sociopathy, the condition of narcissism is particularly interesting and instructive. Narcissism is, in a metaphorical sense, one half of what sociopathy is. Even clinical narcissists are able to feel most emotions as strongly as anyone else does, from guilt and sadness to desperate love and passion. The half that is missing is the crucial ability to understand what other people are feeling. Narcissism is a failure not of conscience but of empathy, which is the capacity to perceive emotions in others and so react to them appropriately. The poor narcissist cannot see past his own nose, emotionally speaking, and as with the Pillsbury Doughboy, any input from the outside will spring back as if nothing had happened. Unlike sociopaths, narcissists often are in psychological pain, and may sometimes seek psychotherapy. When a narcissist looks for help, one of the underlying issues is usually that, unbeknownst to him, he is alienating his relationships on account of his lack of empathy with others, and is feeling confused, abandoned, and lonely. He misses the people he loves, and is ill-equipped to get them back. Sociopaths, in contrast, do not care about other people, and so do not miss them when they are alienated or gone, except as one might regret the absence of a useful appliance that one had somehow lost.

For their own reasons, sociopaths sometimes marry, but they never marry for love. They cannot fall genuinely in love, not with their spouses, their children, or even a pet. Clinicians and researchers have remarked that where the higher emotions are concerned, sociopaths can "know the words but not the music." They must learn to appear emotional as you and I would learn a second language, which is to say, by observation, imitation, and practice. And just as you or I, with practice, might become fluent in another language, so an intelligent sociopath may become convincingly fluent in "conversational emotion." In fact, this would seem to be only a mildly challenging intellectual task, quite a lot easier than learning French or Chinese. Any person who can observe human actions even superficially, or who can read novels and watch old movies, can learn to act romantic or interested or softhearted. Virtually anyone can learn to say "I love you," or to appear smitten and say the words, "Oh my! What a cute little puppy!" But not all human beings are capable of experiencing the emotion implied by the behavior. Sociopaths never do.

Nurture

Still, as we know from the study of so many other human characteristics, genetic predispositions and neurobiological differences do not comprise unavoidable destinies. The genetic marble of our lives predates our birth, but after we are delivered, the world takes up its sculptress's knife and begins to chisel with a vengeance, upon whatever material nature has provided. Heritability studies tell us that for sociopathy in particular, biology is half of the story at most. In addition to genetic factors, there are environmental variables that affect the condition of being without conscience, though, as we are about to see, just what these influences are remains somewhat obscure.

The speculation about social factors that makes the most immediate, intuitive sense is childhood abuse. Perhaps some people with a genetic and neurological predisposition to sociopathy ultimately become sociopathic, while others do not, because the ones who become sociopaths are abused in childhood, and the abuse worsens their psychological status and possibly even their already compromised neurological functioning. After all, we know as a certainty that childhood abuse has a large number of other negative outcomes, among them run-of-the-mill (nonsociopathic) juvenile delinquency and violence, adult depression, suicidality, dissociation and various divisions of consciousness, anorexia, chronic anxiety, and substance abuse. Psychological and sociological studies show us beyond the shadow of a doubt that childhood abuse is unrelentingly toxic to the psyche.

But the problem with attributing sociopathy to early abuse is that, quite unlike nonsociopathic juvenile delinquency and ordinary violent behavior, there is no convincing body of findings linking the core characteristic of sociopathy—that is, the absence of conscience—with childhood maltreatment. Furthermore, sociopaths as a group are not afflicted with the other tragic consequences of childhood abuse, such as depression and anxiety, and we know from a substantial accumulation of research evidence that survivors of early abuse, whether they be lawbreaking or not, are predictably plagued by such problems.

In fact, there is some evidence that sociopaths are influenced *less* by their early experience than are nonsociopaths. In Robert Hare's diagnostic and statistical studies of American prison inmates, for example, for prisoners who were diagnosed as psychopaths, using the *Psychopathy Checklist* developed by Hare, quality of family life in childhood had no effect whatsoever on the timing of criminal behavior. Whether their family life had been stable or not, those diagnosed as psychopaths first appeared in court at an average age of fourteen. In contrast, for inmates who were not diagnosed as psychopaths (prisoners whose underlying personality structures were more normal), the age at which criminal behavior began was strongly linked with quality of family background. Those with a more stable past first appeared in court at an average age of twenty-four, and those with a troubled background came to court for the first time at about fifteen. In other words, a hardscrabble existence nurtures and hastens ordinary criminal activity, just as one might expect, but the criminality that results from the remorselessness of sociopathy has the appearance of flowering all by itself, and according to its own timetable.

Still searching for environmental influences on the development of sociopathy, many investigators have turned to the concept of *attachment disorder*, rather than childhood abuse per se. Normal attachment is an innate system in the brain that motivates an infant to seek the nearness of her parent, or whatever caregiver is available, so that the very first interpersonal relationship can be formed. This first relationship is crucial not only for reasons of infant survival but also because it allows the infant's immature limbic system to "use" the mature functions of the adult's brain to organize itself. When a parent reacts empathically to an infant, the child's positive emotions, such as contentment and elation, are encouraged, and her potentially overwhelming negative emotions, such as frustration and fear, can be moderated. This arrangement promotes a sense of order and safety that will eventually be encoded in the baby's own memory, providing her with a portable version of what John Bowlby referred to in *Attachment and Loss* as a "secure base" in the world.

Research tells us that adequate attachment in infancy has many happy outcomes, including the healthy development of emotional self-regulation, autobiographical memory, and the capacity to reflect upon one's own experiences and actions. Perhaps most important, attachment in infancy allows the individual to create affectionate bonds with other people later on. The earliest attachments are formed by seven months of age, and most human infants succeed in becoming attached to a first caregiver in a way that develops these important capabilities.

Attachment disorder is a tragic condition that occurs when attachment in infancy is disrupted, because of parental incompetence (as in serious emotional disorder on the part of the parent) or because the infant is simply left too much alone (as in an old-fashioned orphanage). Children and adults with severe attachment disorder, for whom attachment was not possible during the first seven months of life, are unable to bond to others emotionally, and are thereby directed to a fate that is arguably worse than death. In the extreme case, as was discovered in the United States in the ultrahygienic orphanages of the nineteenth and early twentieth centuries, infants who are not touched at all, for purposes of antiseptic perfection, are prone to die quite literally. Succumbing mysteriously to a condition then referred to as *marasmus,* a Greek word that means "wasting away"—a disorder now called "nonorganic failure to thrive"—nearly all of the untouched babies in these orphanages perished. In the intervening hundred years, developmental psychologists and pediatricians have learned that it is crucially important to hold, cuddle, talk to, and caress babies, and that the consequences of not doing so at all are heartbreaking.

In Western Europe and in the United States (which, ironically, is one of the least tactile societies on earth), the grief and loss that attachment disorder can bring was personally experienced by many families during the compassionate rush in the early 1990s to adopt orphaned children from Romania. In 1989, when the Communist regime in Romania fell, horrifying photographs were released to the rest of the world of the hundreds of orphanages that had been kept secret by the psychopathic dictator Nicolae Ceauşescu. Under his regime, Romania was a nation of nearly unsurvivable poverty, and yet Ceauşescu had prohibited both abortion and birth control. Hundreds of thousands of starving children resulted, and nearly 100,000 orphaned children ended up in state-run institutions. Overall in these orphanages, the ratio of orphans to staff was about forty to one. Conditions were grotesquely unsanitary, and except for being given enough food to keep most of them alive, the babies and children were ignored.

The kindest solution seemed to be for affluent foreigners to adopt as many of these children as possible. Well-meaning Western Europeans and North Americans brought Romanian babies into their homes and lovingly tried to nurse them to health. And then a couple in Paris would discover that their beautiful ten-month-old Romanian daughter was inconsolable, and only screamed louder when they tried to hold her. Or a couple in Vancouver would walk into their three-year-old son's bedroom, to find that he had just hurled the new kitten out the window. Or parents in Texas would finally have to admit to themselves that they could not keep their adoptive five-year-old son from spending his days staring into a corner, and that he sometimes viciously attacked their other children in the middle of the night as they slept. Western Europe and North America had imported an attachment disorder nightmare created by a sadistic Romanian sociopath who was no longer even alive. Having been completely deprived of attachment in infancy, many of these rescued children were loveless.

In June 2001, the new leadership of Romania ordered a ban on foreign adoptions, not out of humanitarian concern, but for political and financial reasons. The European Union had just pronounced that impoverished Romania, with its outflow of orphans, had become a "marketplace for children," and would be unlikely to achieve membership in the prosperous fifteen-nation union unless the politically incorrect out-of-country adoptions were terminated. At this writing, more than forty thousand children—a small city's worth—

still live in institutions in the Republic of Romania, which is angling for EU membership in 2007.

Especially since the exposure of the Romanian orphan crisis, psychologists have wondered whether attachment disorder might be the environmental root of sociopathy. The similarities are obvious. Children who suffer from attachment disorder are impulsive and emotionally cold, and are sometimes dangerously violent toward their parents, siblings, playmates, and pets. They tend to steal, vandalize, and start fires, and they often spend time in detention facilities when they are young and in jail when they become adults, just like sociopaths. And children with severe attachment disorders are the only children who are almost as fundamentally scary to us as young sociopaths are.

These similarities have been noticed in many parts of the world. In Scandinavian child psychiatry, for example, a condition called "early emotional frustration" is thought to be caused by a lack of mutual bonding between mother and child, and in Scandinavia, this diagnostic term (*early emotional frustration*) is used to flag a child's greater than average chance of developing a sociopathic character disorder by adulthood. Early emotional frustration is statistically linked to factors that may make mother-infant attachment more difficult, such as preterm birth, extremely low birth weight, and maternal substance abuse during pregnancy.

There are some minor design problems in this kind of research. For instance, certain factors, such as maternal substance abuse during pregnancy, could easily implicate sociopathic mothers, and therefore a return to the genetic explanation. But the major problem with the equation of attachment disorder and sociopathy, despite the scientifically tempting commonalities of the two, is their persistent and undeniable *dissimilarity* with respect to the trademark features of sociopathy. Quite unlike sociopaths, children and adults afflicted with attachment disorders are seldom charming or interpersonally clever. On the contrary, these unfortunate individuals are typically somewhat off-putting, nor do they make any great efforts to "fake" being normal. Many are isolates. Their emotional presentation is flat and uninviting, or sometimes directly hostile, and they tend to swing between the distinctly nonseductive extremes of belligerent indifference and unmeetable neediness. None of this allows in any way for the chameleonlike manipulations and con games of the sociopath, with his smiling deceptions and disarming charisma, or for the intermittent success in the material world that the rather sociable sociopath often achieves.

Many clinicians and parents have reported that sociopathic children refuse to form warm relationships with family members. They tend to pull away, both emotionally and physically. And, of course, so do children with attachment disorders. But very unlike the situation with the sad attachment disorder child, detachment from family is much more likely to be a *result* of the young sociopath's way of being in the world than it is to be the cause of it.

And so, in summary, we have some idea of what one of the underlying neurobiological deficits in sociopathy may be. The sociopaths who have been studied reveal a significant aberration in their ability to process emotional information at the level of the cerebral cortex. And from examining heritability studies, we can speculate that the neurobiological underpinnings of the core personality features of sociopathy are as much as 50 percent heritable. The remaining causes, the other 50 percent, are much foggier. Neither childhood maltreatment nor attachment disorder seems to account for the environmental contribution to the loveless, manipulative, and guiltless existence that psychologists call sociopathy. How nongenetic factors affect the development of this profound condition, and they almost certainly do have an effect, is still mainly a puzzle. The question remains: Once a child is born with this limiting neurological glitch, what are the environmental factors that determine whether or not he will go on to display the full-fledged symptoms of sociopathy? And at present, we simply do not know.

Culture

It is entirely possible that the environmental influences on sociopathy are more reliably linked with broad cultural characteristics than with any particular child-rearing factors. Indeed, relating the occurrence of sociopathy to cultures has so far been more fruitful for researchers than looking for the answer in specific child-rearing variables. Instead of being the product of childhood abuse within the family, or of attachment disorder, maybe sociopathy involves some interaction between the innate neurological wiring of individuals and the larger society in which they end up spending their lives.

This hypothesis is bound to be disappointing to some people, because though altering the conditions of pregnancy, childbirth, and child treatment on a massive scale would be no small project, changing the values and belief systems of an entire culture is an even more gigantic undertaking, with a time horizon that seems distant and discouraging. We might feel a little less daunted if we were to identify a set of child-rearing practices that we could try to correct in our lifetimes. But perhaps society is the true parent of certain things, and we will eventually find that, as William Ralph Inge said in the early twentieth century, "The proper time to influence the character of a child is about 100 years before he is born."

From recorded observations, we do know that sociopaths, by various names, have existed in all kinds of societies, worldwide and throughout history. As an illustration, psychiatric anthropologist Jane M. Murphy describes the Inuit concept of *kunlangeta,* which refers to a person whose "mind knows what to do but does not do it." Murphy writes that in northwest Alaska, *kunlangeta* "might be applied to a man who, for example, repeatedly lies and cheats and steals things and does not go hunting, and, when the other men are out of the village, takes sexual advantage of many women." The Inuits tacitly assume that *kunlangeta* is irremediable. And so, according to Murphy, the traditional Inuit approach to such a man was to insist that he go hunting, and then, in the absence of witnesses, push him off the edge of the ice.

Though sociopathy seems to be universal and timeless, there is credible evidence that some cultures contain fewer sociopaths than do other cultures. Intriguingly, sociopathy would appear to be relatively rare in certain East Asian countries, notably Japan and China. Studies conducted in both rural and urban areas of Taiwan have found a remarkably low prevalence of antisocial personality disorder, ranging from 0.03 percent to 0.14 percent, which is not none but is impressively less than the Western world's approximate average of 4 percent, which translates to one in twenty-five people. And disturbingly, the prevalence of sociopathy in the United States seems to be increasing. The 1991 Epidemiologic Catchment Area study, sponsored by the National Institute of Mental Health, reported that in the fifteen years preceding the study, the prevalence of antisocial personality disorder had nearly doubled among the young in America. It would be difficult, closing in on impossible, to explain such a dramatically rapid shift in terms of genetics or neurobiology. Apparently, cultural influences play a very important role in the development (or not) of sociopathy in any given population.

Few people would disagree that, from the Wild West of the past to the corporate outlaws of the present, American society seems to allow and even encourage me-first attitudes devoted to the pursuit of domination. Robert Hare writes that he believes "our society is moving in the direction of permitting, reinforcing, and in some instances actually valuing some of the traits listed in the *Psychopathy Checklist*—traits such as impulsivity, irresponsibility, lack of remorse." In this opinion he is joined by theorists who propose that

North American culture, which holds individualism as a central value, tends to foster the development of antisocial behavior, and also to disguise it. In other words, in America, the guiltless manipulation of other people "blends" with social expectations to a much greater degree than it would in China or other more group-centered societies.

I believe there is a shinier side of this coin, too, one that begs the question of why certain cultures seem to encourage prosocial behavior. So much against the odds, how is it that some societies have a positive impact on incipient sociopaths, who are born with an inability to process interpersonal emotions in the usual way? I would like to suggest that the overriding belief systems of certain cultures encourage born sociopaths to compensate cognitively for what they are missing emotionally. In contrast with our extreme emphasis on individualism and personal control, certain cultures, many in East Asia, dwell theologically on the interrelatedness of all living things. Interestingly, this value is also the basis of conscience, which is an intervening sense of obligation rooted in a sense of connectedness. If an individual does not, or if neurologically he cannot, experience his connection to others in an emotional way, perhaps a culture that insists on connectedness as a matter of belief can instill a strictly cognitive understanding of interpersonal obligation.

An intellectual grasp of one's duties to others is not the same attribute as the powerfully directive emotion we call conscience, but perhaps it is enough to extract prosocial *behavior* from at least some individuals who would have behaved only in antisocial ways had they been living in a society that emphasized individualism rather than interrelatedness. Though they lack an internal mechanism that tells them they are connected to others, the larger culture insists to them that they are so connected—as opposed to our culture, which informs them resoundingly that their ability to act guiltlessly on their own behalf is the ultimate advantage. This would explain why a Western family by itself cannot redeem a born sociopath. There are too many other voices in the larger society implying that his approach to the world is correct.

As a tiny example, had Skip the American been born into a strongly Buddhist culture, or Shinto, would he have killed all those frogs? Perhaps, or perhaps not. His brain would have been the same, but all the people around him would have maintained that respect for life was necessary. Everyone in his world would have been of the same mind, including his wealthy parents, his teachers, his playmates, and maybe even the celebrities he saw on television. Skip would still have been Skip. He would have felt no honor for the frogs, no guilt if he murdered them, no repugnance, but he might have refrained from doing so because his culture had unanimously taught him a lesson, something on the order of proper table manners, about how to fit in—a lesson that his perfectly good intellect had mastered. Sociopaths do not care about their social world, but they do want, and need, to blend in with it.

Of course, I am implying that our own culture would teach a child like Skip that he could torture small animals and still be passably disguised among us, and regretfully, I think this reflects a fair assessment of our current plight.

Warriors

Within the context of human society as a whole, across all cultures, is there anything about the lack of caring and the absence of conscience that could be considered positive, or at least useful? As it happens, from a certain point of view, there is one such thing. Whether the victim be a frog or a person, sociopaths can kill without experiencing anguish; thus, people who have no conscience make excellent, unambivalent warriors. And nearly all societies—Buddhist, Shinto, Christian, or purely capitalist—make war.

To some extent, we can think of sociopaths as being shaped and maintained by society because nations so often require cold-blooded killers, from anonymous foot soldiers to the conquerors who have made, and continue to make, human history. Sociopaths are fearless and superior warriors, snipers, undercover assassins, special operatives, vigilantes, and hand-to-hand specialists, because they experience no horror while killing (or while ordering killing) and no guilt after the deed is done. By far most people—the bulk of our armies—cannot be so emotionless, and if they are not carefully conditioned, most normal people make fourth-rate killers at best, even when taking the lives of other people is deemed to be necessary. A person who can look another person in the eye and calmly shoot him dead is unusual, and in war, valuable.

Strangely, some acts are so emotionally bankrupt that they *require* the absence of conscience, just as astrophysics requires intelligence and art requires talent. Of warriors who can operate without conscience, Lt. Col. Dave Grossman writes, in *On Killing*, "Whether called sociopaths, sheepdogs, warriors, or heroes, they are there, they are a distinct minority, and in times of danger a nation needs them desperately."

But these same nations pay a concealed price within their borders for the glory they bestow on their steel-cold killers in the field. The path to such glory does not go unnoticed by others for whom guiltless killing is a special aptitude, others who will never find themselves working behind enemy lines. The self-appointed remain at home, among the rest of us, and mainly invisible. From Rambo to Baghdad, the glorification of killing—the glamorizing of the deepest infraction of normal conscience—has been a lasting feature of our mainstream culture, and may well be the most pernicious environmental influence of all on the vulnerable sociopathic minds in our midst. The owner of such a mind does not necessarily kill, but as we are about to find in the next chapter, when he does, he is not always the person one would have suspected.

EIGHT

the sociopath next door

It may be that we are puppets—puppets controlled by the strings of society. But at least we are puppets with perception, with awareness. And perhaps our awareness is the first step to our liberation.

—*Stanley Milgram*

"I wanted to talk to someone, and I think it's because my father's in prison." Hannah, the pretty, thin-lipped twenty-two-year-old who was my new patient, directed this barely audible remark to her right, toward one of my bookshelves. After a moment, she looked at me directly, shyly, and repeated herself: "I need someone to talk to. My father's in prison."

She made a tiny gasp, as if the effort of this much speech had exhausted her lungs, and then she was silent.

Especially when people are very frightened, a certain amount of doing therapy is simply knowing how to paraphrase the comments of the person seated before you without sounding judgmental, or patronizing. I bent forward slightly, my fingers laced around my knee, and tried to recapture Hannah's gaze, which had now dropped to the rust-colored Oriental rug between our chairs.

I said quietly, "Your father's in prison?"

"Yes." She looked up slowly when she answered, almost surprised, as if I had gleaned this information telepathically. "He killed a man. I mean, he didn't mean to, but he killed a man."

"And now he's in prison?"

"Yes. Yes, he is."

She blushed, and her eyes filled.

I am always impressed by the fact that even the tiniest amount of being listened to, the barest suggestion of the possibility of kind treatment, can bring such an immediate rush of emotion. I think this is because we are almost never really listened to. In my work as a psychologist, I am reminded every day of how infrequently we are heard, any of us, or our actions even marginally understood. And one of the ironies of my "listening profession" is its lesson that in many ways, each of us ultimately remains a mystery to everyone else.

"How long has your father been in prison?" I asked.

"About forty-one days. There was a really long trial. They didn't keep him in prison during the trial."

"And you felt that you needed to talk to someone?"

"Yes. I can't . . . It's just so . . . Depressed. I think I'm getting depressed. I have to start med school."

"Med school? You mean in September?"

It was July.

"Yes. I wish I didn't have to."

The tears came, soundless ones, no weeping noises, as if the rest of her were unaware she was crying. Streams fell from her eyes and rolled down onto her white silk shirt, making translucent stains. Apart from this, her demeanor remained unchanged, stoic. Her face did not fall.

I am always moved by stoicism. Hannah's was extreme. I was hooked.

Using both forefingers, she shoved her straight black hair into submission behind her ears. Her hair was so shiny it looked as if someone had polished it. She gazed past me, at the window, and asked, "Do you know what it's like for your father to be in prison?"

"No, I don't," I said. "Maybe you'll tell me."

And so Hannah told me her story, or this part of it.

Her father had been the principal of the public high school in the middle-class suburb where Hannah was raised, in a different state, a thousand miles west of Boston. According to Hannah, he was an extremely likable man who naturally drew people to him—a "star," as Hannah put it—and was much loved by the students, the teachers, and nearly everyone else in the small community that surrounded the high school. He was always at the cheerleading practices and the football games, and whether or not the home team won was personally important to him.

Born and raised in the rural Midwest, he had "strong conservative values," Hannah said. He believed in patriotism and a mightily defended country, and also education and self-betterment. Hannah was his only child, and for as long as she could remember, he had told her that, even though she was not a boy, she could be whatever she wanted to be. Girls could be whatever they wanted to be. Girls could be doctors. Hannah could be a doctor.

Hannah loved her father dearly. "He's the sweetest, most moral man in the world. He really *is,*" she told me. "You should have seen all the people who came to the trial. They just sat there and cried for him, cried and cried. They felt so sorry for him, but there was nothing they could do. You know? Nothing they could do."

The killing took place on a March night when Hannah, a college sophomore at the time, happened to be home on spring break. In the wee hours, she had been wakened by a very loud noise outside her parents' house.

"I didn't know it was a gun until later," she told me.

She got up sleepily to look around, and found her mother standing just inside the open front door of the house, weeping and wringing her hands. The March air was rushing in.

"You know, it's the weirdest thing. I can still close my eyes and see her standing there like that—the wind was blowing her bathrobe around—and it was like I knew everything, everything that happened, right at that moment, before I even knew anything. I knew what had happened. I knew my father would be arrested. I saw it all. Well, that's like a picture from a nightmare, right? The whole thing was like a nightmare. You can't believe it's happening in real life, and you keep thinking you'll wake up. Sometimes I still think I'm just going to wake up, and everything was just some kind of horrible dream. But how did I know everything before I even knew anything? I saw my mom standing there like . . . like it was happening in the past, like déjà vu or something. It was weird. Or maybe not. Maybe it just seems that way now, when I remember it. I don't know."

As soon as she saw Hannah, her mother grabbed her, as if pulling her daughter out of the way of an oncoming train, and screamed at her, "Don't go out there! Don't go out there!" Hannah made no move toward the outside, nor did she press her mother for an explanation. She just stood there in her terrified mother's embrace.

"I'd never seen her like that before," Hannah said. "Still, like I keep wanting to say, it was almost as if I'd been through it already. I knew I'd better stay inside."

At some point—Hannah is not sure how long this took—her father came in by the wide-open front door, to the place where she and her mother stood clutching each other.

"He didn't have the gun in his hand. He dropped it out there in the yard somewhere."

Wearing only pajama pants, he stood before his little family.

"He looked fine. He was sort of panting, but I mean he didn't look frightened or anything, and for just a second, just about half a second, I thought maybe everything was going to be okay."

As she told me this, Hannah's tears came again.

"But I was too scared to ask him what happened. After a while, Mom let go of me. She went and she called the police. I remember she asked him, 'Is he hurt?' And he said, 'I think so. I think I hurt him really bad.' And then she went into the kitchen and she called the police. That's what you're supposed to do, right?"

"Right," I said. It had not been a rhetorical question.

In bits and pieces, Hannah learned what had happened. Earlier during that awful night, Hannah's mother, always a light sleeper, had heard noises coming from the living room, sounds like breaking glass, and had roused her sleeping husband. There were more noises. The man of the house became convinced there was an intruder to be dealt with, and got out of bed to prepare. Carefully (according to his wife, later)—by only the dim illumination of a tiny book light—he took out the gun box that he kept in the bedroom closet, unlocked it, and loaded the gun. His wife pleaded with him simply to call the police. He never even replied to this entreaty. He hissed at her commandingly, "Stay here!" And still in near darkness, he left for the living room.

Seeing him, or, more likely, hearing him, the prowler fled the house by the front door. Hannah's father gave chase, shot at the man, and "by sheer blind luck," as one of his attorneys would put it later, hit him in the back of the head, killing him instantly. As it happened, the intruder fell on the sidewalk between the lawn and the curb. This meant, technically, that Hannah's father had shot an unarmed man on the street.

Strangely, incredibly, no neighbors came out of their houses.

"Everything was so quiet after. So very, very quiet," Hannah said to me there in my office.

The police arrived quickly after Hannah's mother called them, followed by a few more people and a silent ambulance. Eventually, her father and her mother were taken away to the police station.

"My mother called her sister and my uncle to come stay with me for the rest of the night, just like I was suddenly a little girl all over again. They weren't any help. They were pretty hysterical. I think I just felt really numb."

The next day, and in the following weeks, the situation occupied the local media's interest. The shooting had taken place in a quiet middle-class suburb. The shooter was an ordinary middle-class man with no known history of violence. He had not been drunk, nor had he been using drugs. The dead man was a known felon, a drug addict, and just before he was shot, he had broken into the house through a window. No one except the prosecuting attorney disputed that he was a robber, or that Hannah's father had pursued and shot him because he had been an intruder in the house.

This was a victim's rights case. This was a gun-control case. This was a get-tough-on-crime case. It clearly illustrated the dangers of being a vigilante. Or maybe it demonstrated conclusively that home owners ought to have increased rights. The ACLU got mad, the NRA even more so.

There was a long trial, as Hannah had said, and then an appeal and another long trial. In the end, Hannah's father was convicted of voluntary manslaughter and sentenced to a maximum of ten years in prison. The attorneys said it was more likely to be "only" two or three.

The news of a high school principal sentenced to ten years in prison for shooting a burglar on his front lawn aroused strong emotions. There were protests on all sides: The decision was unconstitutional. It defied common sense and natural law. The convicted man was a dangerous self-appointee and a rights violator. He was an American hero and a family-protector. He was a violent madman. He was a martyr to the cause, to any number of causes.

Through all of this, impossibly, Hannah was going to college, making *A*'s, and applying to medical schools, activities dogmatically insisted upon by her embattled father.

"He just wouldn't allow my life to be ruined by all the 'stupidity.' That's what he said."

And Hannah got into nearly every medical school she applied to, despite her father's predicament. She told me that "if anything, the whole thing probably helped me get in. He was a cause."

Finished with her narrative, Hannah searched through a small leather handbag, found a tissue, and began to blot her cheeks and dab at the streaks on her shirt. This she did even though there was a full box of tissues in plain sight on a little table just at her left elbow.

"So you see, I don't really need 'therapy' exactly. But I really would like to talk to someone. I really don't want to be this depressed when I start med school. I don't know. Do you think it would be all right for me to see you?"

Hannah had affected me with her story, and with her demeanor. I felt tremendous sympathy for her, and I told her so. To myself, I wondered how much help she would actually be able to accept from me, the psychological trauma therapist she had called because she had seen my name in a newspaper article. Out loud, we agreed to meet once a week for a while, so Hannah could have someone to talk to. The medical school she had finally chosen was in Boston, and at her mother's urging she had moved east right after her college graduation, so she could be "settled in" before classes started, and away from the craziness back home. Her mother felt the situation with her husband was "negative" for her daughter. I thought I had seldom heard such an understatement, and I assured Hannah that, yes, it would be all right for her to see me.

After she left, I paced around my office for a minute or two, staring out the tall windows onto Boston's Back Bay, walking over to riffle papers on the wide, cluttered desk, and then returning to the windows, as I often do after a session in which someone has told me a great deal, but not nearly everything. As I paced, I was interested not so much in the legal and political questions of who, what, when, and where, but rather in psychology's perennial question of why.

Hannah had not asked why—as in "*Why* did my father shoot that gun? *Why* didn't he just let the man go?" I reflected that, emotionally, she could not afford to ask why, as the answer might be too unsettling. The entire relationship with her father was at stake. And maybe this was the reason she needed me, to help her navigate through the conceivable answers to this perilous question. Perhaps her father had been caught up in the frenzy of the moment and had shot the gun almost accidentally, hitting the intruder lethally in the head "by sheer blind luck," as the attorney had said. Or perhaps her father had genuinely believed his family was in danger, and his protective instincts had taken him over. Or perhaps Hannah's father, the family man, this ordinary middle-class high-school principal, was a killer.

In subsequent sessions, during that summer and in the fall as Hannah began medical school, she told me more about her father. In the kind of work I do, I often hear about behaviors and events that the patient herself, over her lifetime, has grown used to and thinks of as normal, but that to me sound distinctly abnormal and sometimes alarming. This kind of report is what I soon began to get from Hannah. As she described her father, though she obviously believed she was recounting unremarkable stories, I pieced together the picture of an emotionally cold individual whose mean and controlling actions made me cringe. Also, I became familiar with the understandable haze my intelligent young patient was lost in when it came to seeing her father for what he was.

I discovered that Hannah's father dealt with his pretty wife and his high-achieving daughter more like trophies than human beings, usually ignoring them completely when they were sick or having a difficult time for some other reason. But, lovingly, Hannah reinterpreted her father's callous treatment of her.

"He's really proud of me," she said, "or so I've always thought—and so he can't stand it when I make mistakes. Once when I was in the fourth grade, my teacher sent a note home that I wasn't doing my homework. Dad didn't speak to me for two weeks after that. I know it was two weeks because I had this little calendar—I still have it somewhere—and I marked off the days, one by one. It was as if suddenly I didn't even exist. It was awful. Oh, and another good example, more recent: I was in high school already—*his* high school, you know?—and I got this really huge, ugly blemish on my cheek." She pointed to an empty space on her lovely complexion. "He didn't say a word to me—wouldn't even look at me—for three days. He's such a perfectionist. I guess he wants to show me off, and when something's wrong, he really can't do that. It makes me feel bad about myself sometimes, but I suppose I can understand it, more or less."

Hannah described a time in her childhood when her mother had been critically ill and in the hospital for nearly three weeks. Hannah believed her mother had contracted pneumonia, but she said, "I was really too young to remember much about it." Hannah's aunt had taken her to see her mother during this time. But her father had not visited his wife once while she was hospitalized, and when she returned home, he was angry and agitated, concerned that his pale and weakened wife "might not get her beauty back," as Hannah phrased it.

As for Hannah's pretty mother, "There really isn't much to tell," Hannah told me. "She's sweet and gentle. She always took good care of me, especially when I was little. She likes to garden, and she does a lot of charities and such. She's just a really nice lady. Oh, and she was the homecoming queen when she was in high school. Dad likes to tell people that."

When I pressed Hannah about her mother's reaction to her father's neglectful behaviors, she said, "I don't know. I mean, to be honest, there were things that would've made me really angry if I'd been Mom, but she never said anything. She just kind of goes her own way. Like I said, she's a sweet, gentle lady—that's probably what you'd hear if you asked someone who knows her—and I guess what goes along with that is she never really stands up for herself very much. She certainly never confronts Dad. I mean, I think I'd faint dead away if she ever did that. She's the perfect lady. Her only little flaw, if you could even call it that, is her vanity. She's really beautiful, and I think she knows it, and she spends a lot of time working on her hair and her body and such. I think she sees that as her only power in the world, if that makes any sense."

Hannah looked at me questioningly, and I nodded that I understood what she meant.

"And to give him his due, Dad's really good to her about that. He sends her flowers when he's gone, and he always tells her how beautiful she is. I think that kind of thing must really mean a lot to her."

"He sends her flowers when he's gone?" I asked. "Where does he go?"

When I asked that question—"Where does he go?"—Hannah's composure lost a little ground. She shifted in her chair and said nothing for a moment. Finally she replied, "I don't really know. I know that must sound sort of lame, but I don't. Sometimes he'd come in really late at night, or he'd even be gone for a whole weekend. Mom would get flowers—I mean, really, it was between the two of them. It was just too weird, so I tried to ignore it."

"His absences were weird?"

"Yes, well . . . That's the way I felt. I don't know how Mom feels about it."

"Any guesses about where he went?" I pressed her, probably a little too hard, but it seemed an important point.

"No. I always tried to ignore it," she repeated. Then she began to study my bookshelves again.

The next week, I asked Hannah the conspicuous question of whether her father had ever been physically violent with her or her mother. Had he ever hit them?

She brightened and answered eagerly. "Oh no. He's never done anything like that. I can't even imagine it. In fact, if anyone else ever hurt me or Mom, I think he'd kill them."

I waited an instant for the impact of her words to strike her, but she appeared unaffected. She shifted her position again and reinforced her answer, saying, "No. He never hit us. Nothing like that ever went on at all."

She was unaccountably pleased to answer me in this way, and somehow I was inclined to believe her, that her father had never been physically violent in the context of his family. But after twenty-five years of treating trauma survivors, I have learned that getting hit is actually one of the more bearable ways a person can be assaulted.

I tried a different tack. I said, "I know you love your father, and you need to hold on tight to that love right now. But all relationships have their difficulties. There's nothing about him that you'd change if you could?"

"Yes, that's absolutely right. I do need to hold on to him. And he really deserves to have huge sympathy from everyone, especially now. . . ."

She paused, and craned her neck to look behind her at the double doors to my office. Then she turned back and looked at me for a long moment, as if appraising my motives, and finally said, "But since you want to know what I'd change, there is something, actually."

She made a little humorless laugh and blushed scarlet to the roots of her shimmering black hair.

"What's that?" I asked, as matter-of-factly as I could.

"It's a silly thing, really. It's, well . . . Sometimes he flirts with my friends, sort of, and it really bothers me. Actually, now that I say it out loud, it sounds even more ridiculous. I guess it shouldn't bother me so much. But it really does."

"He flirts with your friends? How do you mean?"

"Since junior high school, more or less . . . Some of my friends are really gorgeous, you know? There's this one in particular, named Georgia. . . . Well anyway, he flirts with them. He winks at them and kind of grabs them and tickles them. And sometimes he makes what I think are really suggestive remarks—like he'll say, 'Going braless today, Georgia?' or something—but I guess I'm misinterpreting. Oh man, now that I'm talking about this out loud, it's like *über*-dumb, don't you think? It probably shouldn't bother me at all."

I said, "If I were in your place, I think it would bother me, a lot."

"You do?" She looked encouraged for a moment, and then sagged. "You know, at the high school Dad runs—the high school I went to—parents have actually claimed that he was 'inappropriate' with their kids. There were three times, I think, or at least those are the ones that I heard about. I remember one time the parents were really steamed. They actually took their kid out of the school. Everybody came to his rescue after that. They thought it was really sad these days that such a good, kind man could be accused of some perverse thing just because he gave one of his students a hug, or whatever."

"And what do you think?"

"I don't know. I'll probably burn in hell or something for admitting this, but the truth is that I don't know—I guess because I've seen him do so much stuff that people could misread really easily. You know? I mean, if you're the principal and you walk up behind some hot-looking sixteen-year-old in the hall and you grab her by the waist, you've got to expect her parents to get a little ticked if they hear about it. I don't know why he doesn't understand that."

This time, Hannah did not ask me to confirm her opinion. She stared at the bookshelves some more, and was silent.

Finally, in a little flood of rushed words, she said, "And you know what else? I've never told this to anyone, and I hope you're not going to think less of me because I'm telling you, but one time this girl I know—I didn't know her very well, but she went to the high school—she came up and sat beside me in the library and started writing notes. She was smiling and she wrote, 'Do you know what your father told me about Central High?' and she passed it to me. I wrote, 'I give up. What?' and she wrote, 'He told me Central was like a sexual cafeteria.' She put sexual cafeteria in big quotes. I was so furious I almost couldn't keep from crying, but I got out of there, and then I didn't know what to do with the piece of paper, so I crumpled it up and I put it in my pocket, and when I got home, I got matches and I burned it in the sink."

The rush of words over, she looked down at the rust-colored carpet.

"I'm so sorry, Hannah. You truly didn't deserve to have that happen to you. You must've been so embarrassed, and so heartbroken. But why did you imagine I'd think less of you for telling me?"

In a voice much younger than her twenty-two years, she answered, "I should've kept it a secret. It's disloyal."

Hannah and I continued our sessions together. At the beginning of many of her appointments, she would tell me about strange phone messages her mother was receiving back home.

"After the night of the burglary, we pretty much stopped being able to answer the phone. There were so many so-called reporters, and so many cranks. At this point, Mom always just lets the machine answer, and if it's somebody she wants to talk to, she can pick up. It's okay, I guess. She just erases the cranks. But lately she's been getting these weird druggie messages. They really upset her. They're freaky—I mean, even freakier than the usual freaks."

"Has she told you what they say?" I asked.

"Sort of. She gets so upset, it's a little hard to make sense of what she's saying to me on the phone, but I think the basic idea is they're accusing Dad of dealing drugs or something. Ridiculous stuff—but it really gets to Mom. She said they were demanding to get some kind of 'information' from the house, or they were going to hurt him. I guess they kept saying something about 'information,' and things about hurting him. But there's nothing in the house, and, I mean, Dad's not there. He's in prison."

"Has your mother notified the police about the messages?"

"No. She's afraid that she'll get Dad in trouble."

For a moment, I could not think of an appropriate reply to this last remark, and when I was silent, Hannah filled in. She said, "I know, I know. It's illogical."

By the end of Hannah's first year in medical school, her mother had received a dozen or so of these incomprehensible and frightening messages, and still neither mother nor daughter had reported them to the police.

In May, Hannah decided she wanted to fly out and visit her imprisoned father. We talked about how emotionally painful such a visit would be for her, but she was determined to go. We had several conversations about her upcoming trip, trying to prepare her for the various situations she might need to handle, and for the feelings she might have when she saw her father in prison. But nothing could have prepared either Hannah or me for what did happen. In retrospect, I believe he must have reached the point of wanting an audience for his gamesmanship, a frame of mind similar to Skip's when he enticed his little sister to the lakeside. I cannot think of any other likely reason that Hannah's father would suddenly have been so forthcoming with his daughter. As for Hannah, she had not told me she intended to be blunt with her father. Perhaps she did not even know this herself beforehand. To my mind, her behavior when she visited the prison is one of the best illustrations I have ever encountered of how much a person can know about another person without consciously knowing that she knows it.

When she got back to Boston, this is what she told me about their conversation. I imagine that more was said, but the following is all that Hannah shared with me. She began somewhat tearfully, describing the harrowing and undignified process of getting into a prison to visit an inmate. Then her tears cleared completely and she told me the rest calmly, with a certain intellectual detachment.

She said, "I was terrified he'd look pathetic and beaten, but he didn't look that way at all. He looked fine. He looked . . . I don't know—*alive* is what I want to say. His eyes were sparkling. I've seen him like that before, but I really didn't expect to see him that way in prison. He seemed glad to see me—he asked me about my grades. I thought he'd ask me about Mom, but he didn't. And so I thought, Why put it off? So I asked him."

She made this statement as if I knew what she meant, and I did not. I said, "You asked him what?"

"I asked him, 'What was that man looking for in the house, Dad?' He said, 'What man?' But I'm sure he knew what I was talking about. He didn't look ashamed or embarrassed or any of that. I said, 'The man you shot.' He didn't even blink. He just said, 'Oh, that man. He was looking for some names. But he didn't find them. I can assure you of that.' "

Hannah had been speaking without looking at me. Now she made eye contact, and said, "Dr. Stout, his expression . . . He looked like we were talking about something that was really *fun* to talk about. I wanted to run out of there, but I didn't."

"I didn't know you were going to do this. You're amazing."

"It was awful," she continued without seeming to hear that I was marveling at her actions. "I said, 'So you knew him?' And he said, 'Of course I knew him. Why would I kill a perfect stranger?' And then he laughed. He *laughed,* Dr. Stout."

Still speaking directly to me, though with considerable emotional distance from the subject matter, she went on: "And then I said, 'Are you involved with heroin?' He didn't really answer that one. He just told me that I was smart. Can you believe that? He told me that I was smart."

She shook her head in disbelief and was silent for a while.

Finally, I prompted her. I said, "Did you ask other questions, Hannah?"

"Yes. Yes, I did ask him. I said, 'Have you ever killed anyone else?' And do you know what he said?"

Then she was silent again.

After a moment, I replied, "No, I don't. What did he say?"

"He said, 'I plead the Fifth.' "

Only then did Hannah cry again, this time without restraint. Her sudden, wrenching grief, for the father she had thought was there, reminded me of a quotation from Emerson, who said that of all the ways to lose a person, death is the kindest.

She wept for a long time, but I was relieved to find that when her tears were finally spent, she was able to turn her thoughts to her own safety. Wiping her face with a handful of tissues from the box, she looked at me and said in a steady voice, "The lawyers are going to get him out, you know. What am I going to do?"

And I heard myself answering, with decidedly more directive maternal ferocity than I am accustomed to using in therapy sessions, "You're going to protect yourself, Hannah."

What Can the Conscience-Bound Do About the Guiltless?

Sociopaths are not few and far between. On the contrary, they make up a significant portion of our population. Though Hannah's experience was especially up close and personal, for any individual living in the Western world to get all the way through life without knowing at least one such person, in some capacity or other, is virtually impossible.

People without conscience experience emotions very differently from you and me, and they do not experience love at all, or any other kind of positive attachment to their fellow human beings. This deficit, which is hard even to ponder, reduces life to an endless game of attempted domination over other people. Sometimes sociopaths are physically violent, as Hannah's father was. Often they are not, preferring to "win" over others by raiding the business world, or the professions, or government—or simply by exploiting one person at a time in parasitic relationships, as Sydney's nonhusband, Luke, did.

At present, sociopathy is "incurable"; furthermore, sociopaths almost never wish to be "cured." In fact, it is likely that, building on the neurobiological configuration of sociopathy, certain cultures, notably our Western one, actively encourage antisocial behaviors, including violence, murder, and warmongering.

These facts are difficult for most people to accept. They are offensive, nonegalitarian, and frightening. But understanding and accepting them as a real aspect of our world is rule number one of the "Thirteen Rules for Dealing with Sociopaths in Everyday Life" that I tell to patients like Hannah, and to other people who are interested in protecting themselves and the people they love.

Here are the thirteen rules:

THIRTEEN RULES FOR DEALING WITH SOCIOPATHS IN EVERYDAY LIFE

1. *The first rule involves the bitter pill of accepting that some people literally have no conscience.*

   These people do not often look like Charles Manson or a Ferengi bartender. They look like us.

2. *In a contest between your instincts and what is implied by the role a person has taken on—educator, doctor, leader, animal lover, humanist, parent—go with your instincts.*

   Whether you want to be or not, you are a constant observer of human behavior, and your unfiltered impressions, though alarming and seemingly outlandish, may well help you out if you will let them. Your best self understands, without being told, that impressive and moral-sounding labels do not bestow conscience on anyone who did not have it to begin with.

3. *When considering a new relationship of any kind, practice the Rule of Threes regarding the claims and promises a person makes, and the responsibilities he or she has. Make the Rule of Threes your personal policy.*

   One lie, one broken promise, or a single neglected responsibility may be a misunderstanding instead. Two may involve a serious mistake. But *three* lies says you're dealing with a liar, and deceit is the linchpin of conscienceless behavior. Cut your losses and get out as soon as you can. Leaving, though it may be hard, will be easier now than later, and less costly.

   Do not give your money, your work, your secrets, or your affection to a three-timer. Your valuable gifts will be wasted.

4. *Question authority.*

   Once again—trust your own instincts and anxieties, especially those concerning people who claim that dominating others, violence, war, or some other violation of your conscience is the grand solution to some problem. Do this even when, or especially when, everyone around you has completely *stopped* questioning authority. Recite to yourself what Stanley Milgram taught us about obedience: At least six out of ten people will blindly obey to the bitter end an official-looking authority in their midst.

   The good news is that having social support makes people somewhat more likely to challenge authority. Encourage those around you to question, too.

5. *Suspect flattery.*

Compliments are lovely, especially when they are sincere. In contrast, *flattery* is extreme and appeals to our egos in unrealistic ways. It is the material of counterfeit charm, and nearly always involves an intent to manipulate. Manipulation through flattery is sometimes innocuous and sometimes sinister. Peek over your massaged ego and remember to suspect flattery.

This "flattery rule" applies on an individual basis, and also at the level of groups and even whole nations. Throughout all of human history and to the present, the call to war has included the flattering claim that one's own forces are about to accomplish a victory that will change the world for the better, a triumph that is morally laudable, justified by its humane outcome, unique in human endeavor, righteous, and worthy of enormous gratitude. Since we began to record the human story, all of our major wars have been framed in this way, on all sides of the conflict, and in all languages the adjective most often applied to the word *war* is *holy.* An argument can easily be made that humanity will have peace when nations of people are at last able to see through this masterful flattery.

Just as an individual pumped up on the flattery of a manipulator is likely to behave in foolish ways, exaggerated patriotism that is flattery-fueled is a dangerous thing.

6. *If necessary, redefine your concept of respect.*

Too often, we mistake fear for respect, and the more fearful we are of someone, the more we view him or her as deserving of our respect.

I have a spotted Bengal cat who was named Muscle Man by my daughter when she was a toddler, because even as a kitten he looked like a professional wrestler. Grown now, he is much larger than most other domestic cats. His formidable claws resemble those of his Asian leopard-cat ancestors, but by temperament, he is gentle and peace-loving. My neighbor has a little calico who visits. Evidently, the calico's predatory charisma is huge, and she is brilliant at directing the evil eye at other cats. Whenever she is within fifty feet, Muscle Man, all fifteen pounds of him to her seven, cringes and crouches in fear and feline deference.

Muscle Man is a splendid cat. He is warm and loving, and he is close to my heart. Nonetheless, I would like to believe that some of his reactions are more primitive than mine. I hope I do not mistake fear for respect, because to do so would be to ensure my own victimization. Let us use our big human brains to overpower our animal tendency to bow to predators, so we can disentangle the reflexive confusion of anxiety and awe. In a perfect world, human respect would be an automatic reaction only to those who are strong, kind, and morally courageous. The person who profits from frightening you is not likely to be any of these.

The resolve to keep respect separate from fear is even more crucial for groups and nations. The politician, small or lofty, who menaces the people with frequent reminders of the possibility of crime, violence, or terrorism, and who then uses their magnified fear to gain allegiance, is more likely to be a successful con artist than a legitimate leader. This too has been true throughout human history.

7. *Do not join the game.*

Intrigue is a sociopath's tool. Resist the temptation to compete with a seductive sociopath, to outsmart him, psychoanalyze, or even banter with him. In addition to reducing yourself to his level, you would be distracting yourself from what is really important, which is to protect yourself.

8. *The best way to protect yourself from a sociopath is to avoid him, to refuse any kind of contact or communication.*

   Psychologists do not usually like to recommend avoidance, but in this case, I make a very deliberate exception. The only truly effective method for dealing with a sociopath you have identified is to disallow him or her from your life altogether. Sociopaths live completely outside of the social contract, and therefore to include them in relationships or other social arrangements is perilous. Begin this exclusion of them in the context of your own relationships and social life. You will not hurt anyone's feelings. Strange as it seems, and though they may try to pretend otherwise, sociopaths do not have any such feelings to hurt.

   You may never be able to make your family and friends understand why you are avoiding a particular individual. Sociopathy is surprisingly difficult to see, and even harder to explain. Avoid him anyway.

   If total avoidance is impossible, make plans to come as close as you can to the goal of total avoidance.

9. *Question your tendency to pity too easily.*

   Respect should be reserved for the kind and the morally courageous. *Pity* is another socially valuable response, and it should be reserved for innocent people who are in genuine pain or who have fallen on misfortune. If, instead, you find yourself often pitying someone who consistently hurts you or other people, and who actively campaigns for your sympathy, the chances are close to 100 percent that you are dealing with a sociopath.

Related to this—I recommend that you severely challenge your need to be *polite* in absolutely all situations. For normal adults in our culture, being what we think of as "civilized" is like a reflex, and often we find ourselves being automatically decorous even when someone has enraged us, repeatedly lied to us, or figuratively stabbed us in the back. Sociopaths take huge advantage of this automatic courtesy in exploitive situations.

Do not be afraid to be unsmiling and calmly to the point.

10. *Do not try to redeem the unredeemable.*

Second (third, fourth, and fifth) chances are for people who possess conscience. If you are dealing with a person who has no conscience, know how to swallow hard and cut your losses.

At some point, most of us need to learn the important, if disappointing, life lesson that, no matter how good our intentions, we cannot control the behavior—let alone the character structures—of other people. Learn this fact of human life, and avoid the irony of getting caught up in the same ambition he has—to control.

If you do not desire control, but instead want to *help* people, then help only those who truly want to be helped. I think you will find this does not include the person who has no conscience.

The sociopath's behavior is not your fault, not in any way whatsoever. It is also not your mission. *Your mission* is your own life.

11. *Never agree, out of pity or for any other reason, to help a sociopath conceal his or her true character.*

"Please don't tell," often spoken tearfully and with great

gnashing of teeth, is the trademark plea of thieves, child abusers—and sociopaths. Do not listen to this siren song. Other people deserve to be warned more than sociopaths deserve to have you keep their secrets.

If someone without conscience insists that you "owe" him or her, recall what you are about to read here: "You owe me" has been the standard line of sociopaths for thousands of years, quite literally, and is still so. It is what Rasputin told the empress of Russia. It is what Hannah's father implied to her after her eye-opening conversation with him at the prison.

We tend to experience "You owe me" as a compelling claim, but it is simply not true. Do not listen. Also, ignore the one that goes, "You are just like me." You are not.

12. *Defend your psyche.*

Do not allow someone without conscience, or even a string of such people, to convince you that humanity is a failure. Most human beings *do* possess conscience. Most human beings *are* able to love.

13. *Living well is the best revenge.*

Epilogue

I still meet with Hannah occasionally.

Her father was paroled from prison, but she has not seen him, or even spoken with him, in the last six years. This loss, and the reasons for it, remain a source of tremendous sadness for her.

Her mother and father are now divorced, due not to his violent criminal activities, which Hannah's mother and the rest of society still refuse to acknowledge, but to the fact that she found him in bed with a nineteen-year-old former student.

In testimony to her intelligence and her strength, Hannah finished medical school with honors. But she soon discovered the obvious—that being a doctor had been her father's ambition for her, not her own. He had considered this to be the height of prestige.

Against the odds, Hannah has held on to her ability to feel close to people who are loving and trustworthy, and also on to a dry sense of humor. When she left medicine, for example, she told me she had realized that the medical oath, "First, do no harm," simply did not fit her father at all.

She applied to and was accepted by several law schools. She chose to attend one that offers a specialization in advocacy and human rights.

NINE

the origins of conscience

Why should any animal, off on its own,
specified and labeled by all sorts of signals as its individual self,
choose to give up its life in aid of someone else?

—*Lewis Thomas*

Since we have it on excellent authority that nature is red in tooth and claw, why are all human beings not killers like Hannah's father? Why do most of us, most of the time, operate according to a seventh sense that directs us not to kill, even when we might profit in some way from doing so? And lesser transgressions, too: Why do we usually feel guilty when we steal, or lie, or hurt other people?

We have already discussed what causes sociopathy, and so it is only fair to address the twin question: What causes conscience? From a certain point of view, this inquiry is not merely parallel; it is actually the better and more baffling question. Since Darwin published *The Origin of Species,* in 1859, much of scientific theorizing has considered that all living things, including human beings, have evolved according to the law of natural selection. According to this law, known more popularly as "the law of the jungle," any characteristic that enhances survival and reproduction (and therefore the continuance of its own genetic components) will tend to remain in the population. If a physical trait or a behavioral tendency bestows this felicitous survival advantage on individuals for countless generations, in many situations and across habitats, it may, incrementally and in the course of time immemorial, become part of the standard genetic blueprint for the species.

According to the law of natural selection, tigers have claws, chameleons change colors, rats avoid open spaces, possums play dead, and apes have big brains because tigers with claws, camouflaged lizards, secretive rodents, playacting possums, and very smart primates tend to survive longer and so make more babies than their peers do. In turn, these babies survive better and reproduce more often than their less fortunate playmates who are not genetically endowed with natural weapons, camouflage techniques, survival-promoting anxiety, theatrical ability, or superior intelligence.

But according to this utterly amoral law of the jungle, of what possible use to the individual members of a predatory species—for human beings are technically predators—are the limitations and interruptions of a powerful moral sense? Imagine, for example, a great white shark with a demanding conscience. How long would she live? What, then, can conceivably be the evolutionary origins of human conscience?

Let us put this extraordinary question another way. Picture people stranded on a small, remote island with limited resources. In the long run, what kind of individual is more likely to survive—an honest, moral person, or someone ruthless like Skip? The kind and empathic Jackie Rubenstein, or Doreen Littlefield? Sydney, or the unremittingly self-involved Luke? Hannah, or Hannah's father? If there were a few others on the island for the survivors to make babies with—and given that sociopathy is at least partially genetically determined—over a great many generations, might we not end up with an island populated mainly by people who possessed no conscience? Then would not this population of sociopaths proceed without a second thought to deplete the island's resources completely, and all die? And if, to the contrary, people with conscience were still to be found on the island, where life was fragile and ruthlessness paid off, what in the natural world could possibly have been fostering their moral sense?

Precisely on account of this seemingly impossible challenge to evolutionary theory, naturalists, sociobiologists, comparative psychologists, and philosophers have long been interested in the origins of unselfishness in humans and in other animals. Whenever we carefully observe the actions of the so-called higher animals, we see an apparently irreconcilable dichotomy between selfish survivalism and intense social interest. And of course, nowhere is this dichotomy more extreme than in the human species. We compete ferociously, and we teach our children to compete. We finance wars and weapons of mass destruction. And we also fund foundations, social welfare programs, and homeless shelters, and try to teach our children—those very same children—to be kind.

Our species has produced both a Napoléon and a Mother Teresa. But according to fundamentalist evolutionary theory, Mother Teresa should never have been born, because neither charity nor a sense of good and evil would seem to have anything at all to do with the law of the jungle. So what is going on here? As David Papineau asked in his *New York Times* review of Matt Ridley's book *The Origins of Virtue*, "If nice guys always finished last when our ancestors were scrabbling around for food on the African savanna, why does morality come so naturally to us now?"

And humans are hardly the only animals who can be unselfish. Thomson's gazelles "stot" (leap up and down conspicuously) when they see a predator, decreasing their chances of individual survival but increasing the chances that the herd will get away. Chimpanzees share their meat, and sometimes even their most valued fruit. According to psychobiologist Frans de Waal, a raven will communicate the precious discovery of a carcass with loud calls to the flock, making itself a standout to wolves.

When it comes to surviving, clearly there is a certain conflict of interest between the individual and the herd/community/flock, and arguments concerning the origin of what evolutionary psychologists call "altruistic behaviors" have generally centered around the *unit of selection* in evolution. Does natural selection "choose" only individuals for survival, or can selection perhaps operate at the level of groups, thus favoring the survival of whole populations over others?

If "survival of the fittest" applies only to the individual as the unit of selection, the evolution of unselfishness is almost impossible to explain, for the same reason that cutthroat Skip, Doreen, Luke, and Hannah's father, as individuals, would indeed be more likely to outlast the rest of us on a desert island. But if the unit of selection is the group as a whole, then a certain amount of altruism can be explained. Quite simply, a group composed of individuals who cooperate and take care of one another is much more likely to survive *as a group* than a collective of individuals who can only compete with or ignore one another. In terms of survival, the successful group will be the one that is operating to some extent as an entity, rather than the group in which every single individual is looking out for number one, to the exclusion of everyone else.

Group selection, and all it implies about our true nature, has been an extremely controversial idea among evolutionists, reflecting the fact that the theory of evolution itself is still evolving. Early theories of group selection assumed the possibility that, in the beginning, there had been cohesive groups of altruistic individuals (mammals that emitted warning behaviors, birds that would signal food to the flock, primates who were generous, and so forth) for group selection to favor in the first place. This poorly explained assumption—aggregations of altruists from the clear blue sky—was irritating to many scholars, who bestowed on it the damning label of weak science.

In 1966, George C. Williams of the University of Chicago published a now-classic text entitled *Adaptation and Natural Selection*, in which he argued that although group selection was theoretically possible, it was unlikely to occur in nature. Williams wrote that neither the group *nor* the individual was the fundamental unit of natural selection, maintaining that the true unit of selection was the gene itself. For creatures that reproduce sexually, as opposed to organisms that generate clones, the gene is the only unit that self-replicates exactly (more or less) through time. Children are not exact copies of their parents, but genes *are* fairly precise replicas of themselves. And so, Williams insisted, the gene must be the only unit that natural selection can efficiently use. In other words, "survival of the fittest" meant survival of the fittest genes (or rather, the information coded in them), not necessarily the survival of the fittest individual animals or groups. For Williams, individuals and groups were there only to serve as temporary environments for genetic information.

And ten years later, in 1976, in a still-popular book called *The Selfish Gene*, Richard Dawkins extended Williams's gene-centered theory and biologist W. D. Hamilton's notion of *kin selection*, which paradoxically reexplains the evolution of unselfish behaviors at the level of the individual by invoking the idea of "selfishness" at the level of the gene. This is a rather strange notion, and deserves some explanation.

Kin selection means that pieces of the individual's genetic blueprint (the only biological aspect of the individual that stands a chance of being "immortal," so to speak) will fare better if the individual guards not only his own survival and reproduction odds but also those of other individuals who share some of his genetic makeup. If he behaves generously and protectively toward his blood relatives, their enhanced survival and reproduction rate will increase the numbers of his own genes in future generations, since his relatives and he have many genes in common.

Of course, the expression "selfish gene" is not intended to imply that DNA is a thinking, feeling thing with its own desires. Dawkins uses "selfish gene" as a metaphor. He means that the characteristics of a species are determined by genes that cause individuals to think, feel, and behave in ways that maximize the existence of those same genes in the gene pool, regardless of the effects of those thoughts, feelings, and behaviors on the individuals themselves. For example, if my brain allows me to form emotional attachments, and I feel so warmly toward my cousins that I share my fruit with all of them, my individual life may be shortened, but on average, the odds that my genes will continue in the population have actually been multiplied, because my genes are shared in part by each of my cousins. And the genes that I have donated to the gene pool by lengthening the lives of my cousins may well include the genes that cause me to feel emotional attachments.

In other words, the genes for emotional attachment are "selfish" in the sense that they exist to enhance their own proliferation, and they do this without regard to the well-being or even the continued existence of the individual creature. As in the famous quotation by Samuel Butler, "A chicken is an egg's way of making another egg."

According to many evolutionists, because we share the greatest percentage of our genetic complement with our parents, our siblings, and our children, kin selection accounts for the fact that we tend to be more selfless toward our parents, siblings, and children than toward more distant relatives and strangers. Furthermore, kin selection explains why we nurture and protect our children despite the fact that doing so lessens our own energies and our individual survival resources. From this vantage point, *conscience* is the genetically programmed mechanism that makes sure we do not ignore the extra little packages of our genetic material that just happen to be walking around on feet other than ours.

As for our genetically designed sense of conscience toward the aforementioned distant relatives and strangers—gene-centered evolutionists propose that their version of natural selection would have favored genes that resulted in "reciprocal altruism," or non-zero-sum (win-win) behaviors such as the division of labor, friend seeking, cooperation, and the avoidance of conflict. These behaviors would be mediated by emotions such as gratitude, compassion, and conscience, and so emotions such as these would have had an advantage where the natural selection of genes was concerned.

But in a revival of the idea of group selection, other evolutionary theorists, among them David Sloan Wilson and Stephen Jay Gould, have implored both the biological and the behavioral sciences to consider that evolution may in fact have taken place on more levels than just the gene-centered one. Naturalist Gould reexamines the evidence from paleontology and maintains that natural selection operates on multiple levels, from the gene to the individual to the group, and even—or especially—the species. In addition, he makes the case that forces operating in a much less incremental fashion than natural selection, and far more rapidly than time immemorial—events that include global or near-global catastrophes—have significantly affected the course of evolution and may do so again.

The various levels of natural selection are likely at odds with one another, particularly with respect to altruistic behaviors and emotions such as conscience. At the level of the gene and also at the level of the group, conscience is adaptive, and natural selection would favor it. But at the level of the individual creature, the *absence* of conscience may sometimes be even more adaptive for survival. In this way, nature would constantly be fostering conscience in most of us, while, at a different level, continually supporting a smaller percentage of individuals who thrive without the neurobiological underpinnings of emotional attachment and conscience.

As evolutionist David Sloan Wilson has said, "There are compelling intellectual and practical reasons to distinguish between behaviors that succeed by contributing to group-level organization and behaviors that succeed by disrupting group-level organization. That is what the words 'selfish' and 'unselfish,' 'moral' and 'immoral' are all about in everyday language." What Wilson describes in this way is the same bewildering and all-too-familiar dichotomy: the majority, who think and feel in terms of minimizing conflict, sharing when necessary, and living out their lives with the people they love, and the minority, who prosper from conflict, and for whom life is no more and no less than a constant competition for dominance.

So we find that even on the most reductionistic biological level, the struggle between good and evil is more ancient than humankind. However, the contest is likely to reach its conclusion with us, and its ultimate resolution will depend on the ways we meet the towering challenges humankind has brought into the world, among them the problem of sociopathy. In ways we are just beginning to understand, natural selection has favored a certain amount of altruism in the human population and has helped to shape a human species endowed with the capacity to love and bond together in positive intention by the still small voice of conscience. At least 96 percent of us are fundamentally thus. What we will end up doing with the species survival problems created by the other 4 percent is, at present, unknowable.

Heinz's Dilemma

Turning now from evolutionary psychology to developmental psychology, we come to the interesting question of how conscience develops in human children. Does conscience flower naturally in children's minds as their other mental abilities increase, or do children acquire and adjust their moral sense as they experience life, from lessons taught by family, society, and culture?

Conscience as an emotion has not been studied in this way, but we can learn much from what is known about its intellectual partner, *moral reasoning.* Moral reasoning is the thought process that attends conscience and helps it decide what to do. If we try, we can express our moral reasoning in words, concepts, and principles.

Joe was engaged in moral reasoning as he drove along in his Audi, along with his tormented conscience, and tried to figure out whether he should go to an important meeting at work or return home to feed his dog, Reebok. *Conscience*, as we know, was Joe's intervening sense of obligation based in his emotional attachment to his dog. *Moral reasoning* was the process by which he determined just what that obligation consisted of, and how to accomplish it. (Exactly how hungry will the dog be? Could he die of thirst? Which is more important, the meeting or Reebok? What is the right thing to do?)

Where does it come from, this nearly universal ability to ask moral and ethical questions of ourselves, about everything from whether or not to feed the dog to whether or not to launch a nuclear missile?

The systematic study of moral reasoning began in the 1930s with Swiss psychologist Jean Piaget. In one of his most influential works, *The Moral Judgment of the Child,* Piaget analyzed children's perspectives on authority, lying, stealing, and the concept of justice. He began by recording detailed observations of how children at different ages conceived of rules and played games, and of how they interpreted moral dilemmas. Piaget's approach was "structural," meaning that he believed human beings developed psychologically and philosophically in a progressive fashion, each cognitive-developmental step building on the previous one, and that the course of this development proceeded in the same order for all children.

Piaget described two general stages of moral development. The first stage is the "morality of constraint," or "moral realism," in which children obey rules because rules are regarded as inalterable. At this black-and-white stage of reasoning, young children believe that a particular deed is either absolutely right or absolutely wrong and that people will inevitably be punished for wrong behavior that is discovered, an expectation Piaget called "imminent justice." The second Piagetian stage is the "morality of cooperation," or "reciprocity." At this stage, children view rules as relative and subject to alteration under certain circumstances, and their concept of justice gives consideration to people's intentions. Older children can "decenter" their point of view (make it less egocentric), and moral rules are understood as important to the functioning of society, rather than only as ways to avoid individual bad outcomes.

Continuing in the Piagetian tradition, and influenced also by the work of the American philosopher John Dewey, psychologist and educator Lawrence Kohlberg began his work on moral judgment in the late 1960s, at Harvard University's Center for Moral Education. Kohlberg's ambition was to discover whether or not there truly were universal stages of moral development.

Kohlberg's theory is based on interviews with boys, ages six to sixteen, in the United States, Taiwan, Mexico, Turkey, and the Yucatán. During these interviews, the children listened to ten stories, each involving a moral dilemma of some kind. The best known of these stories, a little vignette composed nearly forty years ago, is strikingly evocative of the current controversy surrounding pharmaceutical corporations and the cost of prescription medications. It is Heinz's dilemma, which, in paraphrase, is this:

> Heinz's wife is dying from a rare form of cancer. According to the doctors, there is one drug that could save her, a radium compound that a druggist in Heinz's town has recently discovered. The ingredients for the drug are expensive to begin with, and the druggist is charging ten times what it costs him to make the medicine. The druggist pays two hundred dollars for the radium and charges his customers two thousand dollars for a small dose. Heinz goes to everyone he can think of and asks to borrow money. Still, he ends up with only about one thousand dollars. Heinz explains to the druggist that his wife will die without the drug, and asks him to sell the medicine at a cheaper price or to take payment later. But the druggist replies, "No, I discovered the drug, and I'm going to make money from it." Heinz becomes

desperate. He breaks into the druggist's store and steals the drug for his wife.

Should Heinz have done that?

Kohlberg was primarily interested not in the children's yes or no answers to "Should Heinz have done that?" but in the reasoning behind their responses, which he recorded. Based on his many interviews, he proposed that children follow a universal course from self-interest to principled behavior that can be described by a three-level scheme of moral development. The three levels of moral development require increasingly complex and abstract thought patterns, each level displacing the previous one as the child matures cognitively.

According to Kohlberg's theory of moral development, seven- to ten-year-old children reason on the "preconventional level," at which they defer to adult authority and obey rules based only on expectations of punishment and reward. Kohlberg considered that the preconventional reasoning of young children was essentially "premoral." The most typical "premoral" response to Heinz's dilemma would be, "No, Heinz shouldn't have done that, because now he'll be punished."

Beginning at about age ten, children move to the "conventional level" of moral reasoning (conventional in the societal sense), when their behavior is guided by the opinions of other people and a desire to conform. At this level, obeying authority becomes a value in itself, without reference either to immediate rewards and punishments or to higher principles. Kohlberg believed that by the time a child was thirteen, most moral questions were answered on the conventional level. The conventional reasoning about Heinz's theft would be, "No, he shouldn't have stolen the drug. Stealing is against the law. Everyone knows that."

Sometime during adolescence, according to Kohlberg, a few people develop beyond the conventional level to the third and highest level, which he called "postconventional morality." This third level requires the individual to formulate abstract moral principles and to act on them to satisfy his own conscience, rather than to gain the approval of others. At the postconventional level, moral reasoning transcends the concrete rules of society, rules that the individual now understands are often in conflict with one another anyway. His reasoning is informed instead by fluid, abstract concepts such as freedom, dignity, justice, and respect for life. Where Heinz is concerned, a person reasoning at the postconventional level might well insist that human life was more valuable than money, and that the sanctity of life was a moral law that superseded society's rules about stealing. ("Yes, it's a difficult problem, but it's understandable that Heinz would steal the lifesaving drug that the druggist was withholding for reasons of money.")

Kohlberg believed that most people never completely achieved postconventional moral reasoning, even in adulthood, because when he interviewed older boys and young men in his studies, he found that fewer than 10 percent of them offered clear level-three responses. As a footnote here, I would mention that this view of Kohlberg's, if right, might help to explain the passing strange fact that moral outrage from the public is relatively limited when it comes to the aforementioned wealthy pharmaceutical companies. Perhaps most of us, Americans especially, are inclined to accept the druggist's proprietary claim, "I discovered the drug, and I'm going to make money from it." Honoring ownership above all other features of a situation is a part of conventional moral reasoning—or it is at least among men raised in North America.

Enter Gender and Culture

What factor does Kohlberg's system of moral development leave out, even at its highest level? Answer: Heinz's relationship with his spouse, which is appreciably more personal, and perhaps more compelling, than even the most evolved understanding of the general sanctity of life.

And what, most likely, is the major flaw in Kohlberg's overall research design? It is that when he originally asked his moral questions, he asked them only of boys. Kohlberg, a brilliant social scientist, somehow managed to overlook half the human race.

This oversight was addressed in 1982, in a groundbreaking book by Carol Gilligan, entitled *In a Different Voice: Psychological Theory and Women's Development.* A student of Kohlberg's, Gilligan too was interested in advancing a universal stage theory of moral development, but she strongly disagreed with the limited content of the moral levels Kohlberg had proposed. Kohlberg, she said, had produced a model of moral reasoning that was based on an "ethic of justice," a preoccupation with "the rules," be they concrete or abstract. Gilligan believed that Kohlberg had derived only an "ethic of justice" because he had interviewed only males, and that if women were interviewed, a very different system of ideals would emerge. She interviewed women who were making momentous decisions in their lives and discovered that these women were thinking about the *caring* thing to do, rather than pondering "the rules." Women, decided Gilligan, reasoned morally according to an "ethic of care," rather than a male "ethic of justice." She theorized that this was so because girls identify with their mothers and tend to have experiences within the family that emphasize interpersonal responsiveness.

Gilligan argued eloquently that neither vantage point was superior to the other, but that the two ethics simply informed two different voices. Men spoke of attachment to societal and personal rules, and women spoke of attachment to people. Women's moral development, Gilligan said, was based not solely on changes in cognitive capability but also on maturational changes in the way the self and the social environment were perceived.

A woman's postconventional judgment regarding Heinz's dilemma would refer to the importance of his relationship with his wife, and might assert as well that the druggist's claim was immoral because he was allowing someone to die when he could do something to prevent it. Gilligan was persuaded that postconventional reasoning in women focused on the value of doing no harm to self or others, which is more specific and relational, and in many ways more demanding, than a principle such as the general sanctity of life.

Thanks to Carol Gilligan, psychologists and educators now understand that moral reasoning has more than one dimension and that people develop morally in much more complex ways than we first believed. In the last twenty years, newer studies have shown us that both women and men may use both an "ethic of care" and an "ethic of justice" in their moral reasoning. These two voices speak in complex choruses, and gender differences are far more intricate than a single unambiguous line between all women and all men.

We now know also that there are probably no universal stages of moral development through which all human beings everywhere pass, even when we divide the human race in half by gender. Cultural relativism exists even in the moral domain. And if moral reasoning has two dimensions, one of justice and one of care, then why not three dimensions, or hundreds, or more? Why not as many perspectives as there are human situations, values, and ways to raise children?

One illustration of the significance of context and culture in moral judgment is the work of Joan Miller and David Bersoff of Yale University. Miller and Bersoff have studied American children and adults from New Haven, Connecticut, as compared with Hindu children and adults from Mysore City, in southern India. They point out that American culture encourages highly individualistic views of the self—autonomy and personal achievement for both boys *and* girls—versus Hindu Indian culture, which teaches an interdependent concept of the self to both sexes—the value of permanent ties to other people, and of subordinating one's personal ambitions to the goals of the group.

In their studies of moral development, Miller and Bersoff found that Hindu Indians tend to regard interpersonal responsibilities as socially enforceable moral duties, as opposed to the American view of such tasks as occasions for personal decision making. For example, whether or not to take care of one's sister who has Down's syndrome after one's parents can no longer do so would be viewed by an American as a choice, a decision that had moral implications, but a choice nonetheless. The same situation would be seen by a Hindu Indian as a nonnegotiable moral imperative (dharma), along with an expectation that the family would compel the fulfillment of this duty if necessary. Furthermore, Indians believe that interpersonal duty is a natural part of what most individuals are inclined to do anyway, as opposed to Americans, who believe that social expectations and personal wishes are almost always opposed to each other and that one must somehow strike a "balance" between them.

Such differences in belief and early instruction are large, and they tend to create substantial cross-cultural diversity in moral reasoning. Miller and Bersoff report that Hindu Indians, both men and women, develop according to a "duty-based perspective," a dimension of moral judgment that is different from both the "ethic of justice" and the "ethic of care." They conclude, "We interpret our results as implying that qualitatively distinct types of interpersonal moral codes develop in American and Hindu Indian cultures, reflecting the contrasting cultural views of the self emphasized in each setting."

And yet, despite the many and diverse processes of moral judgment spun off by our various human cultures, in the final analysis there is something more to the heart of the matter, something deeper and much less variable. This fixed psychological element is our sense of an irreconcilable contest between moral forces. An overall perception of good and evil as a duality in human life would seem to be completely and astonishingly universal (astonishing to social scientists at least). Good versus evil is the ageless, culture-free human plot, and the undertones of a seemingly universal moral struggle are readily recognized by both genders in all cultures. I would expect a woman from the south of India to possess this fundamental sense of a divided moral realm, and she would expect the same of me. For example, where poor, desperate Heinz is concerned, independent of a judgment regarding how he should resolve his dilemma—what he should or should not *do*—there will be a general, if unspoken, agreement across cultures that Heinz, with his commitment to someone he loves, has the higher moral ground as the story begins, and that the selfish druggist is behaving badly.

There is no global consistency in the intellectual process of moral reasoning itself, in how we think through moral dilemmas and decide what specifically to do. But is there a unity in our emotional reaction to the moral struggle between good and evil, a near-universal seventh sense that can be relied on to ignore all of our differences and borders?

And if so, how does it feel?

The Universal Bond

As I begin to write the final section of this chapter on the origins of conscience, it is the morning of September 11, 2003. I usually like quiet while I work, but this morning I have turned on a television in the other room so that I can hear the voices of the children at the site of the former World Trade Towers as they read the names, one by one, of the people who perished there. Earlier this morning, I sent my daughter off to school, just as I did on the morning of September 11 two years ago. The difference is that two years ago, between the time I sent her to school and the time she came home, the whole world had changed.

I notice how easily the flood of emotion still comes, though two years have gone by since then.

Of all the unexpected reactions a person can have during a catastrophe, one of the more surprising ones for me was feeling suddenly and very consciously linked to all the people I had ever known in my life, from childhood on, everyone who had ever been important to me even for a little while, anyone for whom I had ever felt affection. In the days after September 11, 2001, I remembered people I had not seen or even thought about for years or, in some cases, decades. I saw their faces in my mind with almost unnerving clarity. I had no idea where many of these people were, so long had it been since they were in my life, but I wanted, helplessly, to pick up the phone and call all of them. I wanted to ask them how they were—my high-school writing teacher long ago in North Carolina, a roommate from college, the softhearted proprietor of a grocery where I used to shop in Philadelphia, who would give away food to those who could not afford it and then enjoin his other customers to secrecy. Were they okay? Those whom I could call, I called. No one even found this strange. We simply checked in with one another.

Moral reasoning—the way we think about moral dilemmas—is anything but consistent and universal. It varies with age and with gender. It differs from one culture to the next, and most likely from one region or even one household to the next. For example, what I think about terrorism and what we should do about it will probably be slightly different from what my neighbor thinks, and will almost certainly be different from the beliefs of people who are removed from me by oceans and continents. But in a kind of human miracle, one thing remains constant for nearly all of us—with some notable exceptions—and that is our profound attachment to other human beings. Emotional attachment is part of most of us, down to the very molecules that design our bodies and our brains, and sometimes we are powerfully reminded of it. Beginning in our genes and spiraling outward to all of our cultures, beliefs, and many religions, it is the shadow of the whisper of the beginning of an understanding that we are all one. And whatever its origins, this is the essence of conscience.

TEN

bernie's choice: why conscience is better

Happiness is when what you think, what you say, and what you do are in harmony.

—Mahatma Gandhi

If you could be completely free of conscience—no moral scruples and no guilt at all—what do you think you would do with your life?

When I ask people this question, as I often have, the typical response is, "Oh wow," or "Oh my goodness," followed by a silence during which they wrinkle their faces in mental effort, as if someone had asked them a question in a language they only half-understood. Then most people grin or laugh, seemingly embarrassed by the authority of conscience in their lives, and reply with some version of, "I don't really know what I'd do, but I'm sure it wouldn't be what I'm doing now."

After "Oh wow" and a brief pause, one especially imaginative person chuckled and said, "Maybe I'd be the dictator of a small country or something." He said this as if such an ambition would have been smarter and more impressive than the socially valuable professional career he had in fact pursued.

Would it be smarter not to have a conscience? Would we be happier? We know that groups of people would end up in trouble—whole nations of sociopaths, everyone out for himself or herself alone. But realistically, on a personal level, would you or I, as individuals, be happier and better off if we could shed the limitations of conscience? It would certainly seem so at times. Dishonest people hold positions of power, and corporate thieves purchase Gulfstreams and yachts, while we work responsibly and make "sensible" car payments. But what is the truth of the matter? From a psychological point of view, do sociopaths really have better lives than we do, or is having a conscience somehow the happier fate?

In an ironically utilitarian way, from the beginning, we were selected by nature to be social, sharing creatures, our very brains wired for emotional connectedness with one another, and for a sense of conscience. Or rather, all but a few of us took this path. Profiting from a different but equally businesslike selection process, a few evolved as rogues, apathetic to their brother and sister human beings, with emotionally disconnected brains that hatched thoroughly selfish agendas. Judging from the vantage of the twenty-first century, and looking through the eyes of psychology, which of these two ancient factions, the socially conscientious or the sociopathic, can we say got human nature's better deal?

The Losing Side of Winning

It would be difficult to refute the observation that people who are completely unhampered by conscience sometimes achieve power and wealth, at least for a while. Too many chapters in the human history book, from its first lines to its most contemporary entries, are organized around the stupendous successes of military invaders, conquerors, robber barons, and empire builders. Such individuals are either too long dead or too privileged to be formally evaluated in the fashion a clinical psychologist would like. But given certain of their well-known and highly documented behaviors, we assume, even without knowing their scores on the Pd scale, that a fair number of them would not be found to possess any intervening sense of obligation based in emotional attachment to others. In other words, some of them were, and are, sociopaths.

To make matters worse, brutal conquerors and empire builders are usually held in awe by their contemporaries, and during their lifetimes they are often seen as role models for the entire human race. No doubt countless thirteenth-century Mongol boys were put to bed with tales of the indomitable Genghis Khan, and one wonders which of the modern heroes we tout to our own children will ultimately be remembered by history as motivated by ruthless self-interest.

Sexual conquest also is served rather well by the absence of conscience. To illustrate this point using the offspring of the same famous tyrant, Genghis Khan's eldest son, Tushi Khan, is said to have sired forty sons via his birthright to pick from the most beautiful women of the conquered. The remainder of the vanquished, along with their sons, were routinely slaughtered. One of Genghis's many grandsons, Kublai Khan, founder of the Yuan dynasty, had twenty-two legitimate sons, and added thirty virgins to his harem every year. And as of the time I write these words, virtually identical Y chromosomes are carried by almost 8 percent of the men living in the region of the former Mongol Empire, 16 million of them. Geneticists believe this means that some 16 million people living in the twenty-first century are stamped with Genghis Khan's thirteenth-century legacy of genocide and rape.

Genghis Khan was exceptional among sociopathic tyrants in that he did not die a violent or an ignominious death. Instead, he fell off a horse during a hunt, in 1227. By far most perpetrators of genocide and mass rape eventually take their own lives or are killed, often by enraged followers who have had enough. Caligula was assassinated by one of his own guards. Hitler is believed to have put a pistol in his mouth, and his body is said to have been cremated with diesel fuel. Mussolini was shot and his body hung by its heels in a public square. Romania's Nicolae Ceauşescu and his wife, Elena, were killed by a firing squad in 1989, on Christmas Day. Cambodia's Pol Pot died in a two-room hut, held prisoner by former associates, his body burned under a pile of garbage and rubber tires.

Global sociopaths most typically come to no good end, and this sharply downward tendency is displayed by the more local ones as well. In the final analysis, sociopathy appears to be a losing game, regardless of its scale. Hannah's father, for example, lost everything that should have been precious to him. By the time he was fifty, he had forfeited his job, his position in the community, his beautiful wife, and his loving daughter, all for the exhilaration of being a minor player in the heroin game, and in the end, he is likely to die from a bullet to his own head, from the gun of some other small-time criminal. Luke, my patient Sydney's deadbeat ex, also lost everything that was valuable—his wife, his son, and even his swimming pool. Super Skip, though he blithely deems himself to be too unassailable and too smart to be brought down by the likes of the Securities and Exchange Commission, probably will prove to be neither when the SEC finally sets upon him in earnest. "Dr." Doreen Littlefield, even with a mind fully sharp enough to pursue a real Ph.D., will instead migrate as a fake to more and more obscure locations, playing the same tedious games with the decent people she envies, until she runs out of places to hide. By the time she is fifty, her travels and her unchecked covetousness will have emptied her bank account and pinched her face into that of a bored seventy-year-old.

A list of such dreary endings could go on and on. Contrary to what seems to be a rather popular belief, acting ruthlessly does not, in the end, bring you more than your fair share of the good things in life. Quite the opposite, one might even say that, for the extraordinarily patient observer, one technique to determine whether or not a questionable person is a genuine sociopath is to wait until the end of her life and witness whether or not she has ruined herself, partially or maybe even completely. Does she really possess what you would love to have in your life, or, instead, is she isolated, burned-out, and bored? Is it perhaps stunning the way the mighty have fallen?

Since we began to record wars, occupations, and projects of genocide, historians have often remarked that a certain type of catastrophic, amoral villain seems to be born over and over into the human race. No sooner are we rid of one than another appears somewhere else on the planet. From the point of view of population genetics, there is probably some truth to this legend. And since we do not understand these people, since their psychology is so alien to most of us, we often do not recognize or stop them until after they have damaged humanity in unfathomable ways. But, as Gandhi pointed out with such wonder and relief, "in the end, they always fall—think of it, always!"

The same phenomenon occurs on smaller scales too. Ordinary people without conscience visit pain on their families and communities, but in the end, they tend to self-destruct. Small-time sociopaths would survive long enough to dominate some of the others on our imaginary desert island, maybe promulgate some genes, but at the end of the day, they would probably be hung up by their heels.

Part of the reason for this eventual failure is obvious, especially in cases where infamous despots such as Mussolini or Pol Pot have been killed and mutilated by angry ex-followers. If you oppress, rob, murder, and rape enough people, eventually some of them will gang up on you and take their revenge. We can see this in the much less epic story of Doreen Littlefield as well. The odds were always against her, and finally she just happened to make the wrong person mad. But there are additional reasons, less obvious, for the long-term failure of living without a conscience, reasons that are endemic to the psychology of sociopathy rather than the rage of other people.

And the first of these is boredom, plain and simple.

Is That All There Is?

Though we all know what boredom is, most normal adults do not experience sheer boredom very often. We are stressed, rushed, and worried, but we are seldom purely bored—in part because we are so stressed, rushed, and worried. Time without anything we must attend to usually feels like a breather, not like monotony. To get a feel for what sheer boredom is like, we must hearken back to childhood. Children and adolescents are frequently bored, so bored they can hardly even stand it. Their perfectly normal developmental need for constant stimulation, for exploring and ongoing learning, is often thwarted in a world of long trips, rainy afternoons, and study halls. In childhood, boredom can be excruciating, like a chronic spiritual headache, or a powerful thirst with no beverage to be had. It can hurt so bad that the poor kid feels like yelling out loud, or throwing something noisy at a wall. Extreme boredom is arguably a form of pain.

Lucky for us, adults do not have the same need for constant stimulation. Despite our stresses, we tend to live within a fairly manageable window of arousal, neither unbearably overstimulated nor understimulated—except for sociopaths. People who are sociopaths report that they crave extra stimulation almost continually. Some use the word *addicted*, as in *addicted* to thrills, *addicted* to risk. Such addictions occur because the best (maybe the only) consistent cure for understimulation is our emotional life, so much so that in many psychology texts, the terms *arousal* and *emotional response* are used almost interchangeably. We are stimulated by our meaningful ties to, negotiations with, and happy and unhappy moments alongside other people, and sociopaths do not have this emotional life to live. They do not experience the sometimes harrowing, sometimes thrilling, ever-present arousal that unavoidably attends genuine attachments to other people.

Laboratory experiments using electric shocks and loud noises have found that even the physiological reactions (sweating, racing heart, and so forth) normally associated with anxious anticipation and learned fear are far less pronounced in sociopaths. For adequate stimulation, sociopaths have only their games of domination, and these games get old and stale very quickly. Like drugs, the games have to be done over and over, larger and better, and depending on the resources and talents of the particular sociopath, this may not be possible. And so in sociopathy, the pain of boredom can be nearly constant.

The inclination to dilute boredom chemically for a while is part of the reason sociopaths tend to be alcohol and drug abusers. A major comorbidity study published in 1990 in the *Journal of the American Medical Association* estimates that as many as 75 percent of sociopaths are dependent on alcohol, and 50 percent abuse other drugs. And so sociopaths are often addicts in the usual sense, in addition to being figuratively addicted to risk. With its "peak experiences" and its dangers, the drug culture holds more than one form of appeal for the conscienceless, and the drug culture is where many sociopaths feel most at home.

Another study, published in 1993 in the *American Journal of Psychiatry*, found that 18 percent of intravenous-drug abusers diagnosed with antisocial personality disorder were HIV-positive, while only 8 percent of intravenous-drug abusers without antisocial personality disorder tested positive for HIV. The higher odds ratio of HIV infection among sociopaths is presumably due to their greater risk-taking behaviors.

These statistics bring us back to a question I posed in the first chapter: Is the absence of conscience an adaptive condition, or is it a mental disorder? One operational definition of mental disorder is any psychological condition that causes substantial "life disruption," which is to say, serious and unusual limitations in a person's ability to function as well as might be expected given that person's overall health and level of intelligence. Common sense tells us that the *presence* of any of the recognized mental disorders—major depression, chronic anxiety, paranoia, and so forth—would likely cause woeful "life disruption." But what about the *absence* of something we usually regard as a strictly moral trait? What about the absence of conscience? We know that sociopaths almost never seek treatment, but do they suffer "life disruption" nonetheless?

A way of approaching this issue is to consider what is meaningful in life to the sociopath—winning and domination—and then to ponder the following odd question: Why are all sociopaths *not* in positions of great power? Given their focused motivation, and granted the freedom of action that results from having no conscience whatsoever, they should all be formidable national leaders or international CEOs, or at least high-ranking professionals or dictators of small countries. Why do they *not* win all the time?

For they do not. Instead, most of them are obscure people, and limited to dominating their young children, or a depressed spouse, or perhaps a few employees or coworkers. Not an insignificant number of them are in jail, like Hannah's father, or in danger for their careers or their lives. Very few are fabulously wealthy like Skip. Even fewer are famous. Having never made much of a mark on the world, the majority are on a downward life course, and by late middle age will be burned out completely. They can rob and torment us temporarily, yes, but they are, in effect, failed lives.

From a psychologist's point of view, even the ones in prestigious positions, even the ones with famous names are failed lives. For most of us, happiness comes through the ability to love, to conduct our lives according to our higher values (most of the time), and to feel reasonably contented within ourselves. Sociopaths cannot love, by definition they do not *have* higher values, and they almost never feel comfortable in their own skins. They are loveless, amoral, and chronically bored, even the few who become rich and powerful.

And they are uncomfortable in their skins for more reasons than boredom. The absolute self-involvement of sociopathy creates an individual consciousness that is aware of every little ache and twitch in the body, every passing sensation in the head and chest, and ears that orient with acute personalized concern to every radio and television report about everything from bedbugs to ricin. Because his concerns and awareness are geared exclusively toward himself, the person without conscience sometimes lives in a torment of hypochondriacal reactions that would make even the most fretful anxiety neurotic appear rational. Getting a paper cut is a major event, and a cold sore is the beginning of the end.

Perhaps the most famous historical example of the sociopath's obsession with his body is Adolf Hitler, who was a lifelong hypochondriac with an overpowering fear of developing cancer. In an attempt to keep cancer at bay, and to cure a long list of other imaginary health problems, he swallowed "remedies" formulated specially by his favorite personal physician, Dr. Theodore Morell. Many of these tablets contained hallucinogenic toxins. In this way, Hitler gradually poisoned himself into actual illness. Most likely on account of this, a tremor (a real one) in his right hand became conspicuous, and by mid-1944, he was disallowing photographs.

Sociopaths sometimes use their hypochondriasis as a strategy to get out of doing work. One moment they are fine, but then it is time to pay the bills or look for a job or help a friend move to a new apartment, and suddenly they have chest pains or a limp. And imaginary medical concerns and infirmities often secure special treatment, such as the one last chair in an overcrowded room.

In general, there is an aversion to sustained effort and organized projects of work, and, of course, this preference for ease is extremely self-limiting where success in the real world is concerned. Getting up every single morning and working for a long succession of hours is almost never considered. Sociopaths feel that the easy scheme, the one-shot deal, or the clever ambush is much to be preferred over day-to-day commitment to a job, a long-term goal, or a plan. Even when sociopaths are found in high-status jobs, these positions tend to be those in which the amount of actual hard work done (or not) can be easily obscured, or where others can be manipulated into being the real workers. In such settings, a smart sociopath can sometimes keep things going with an occasional splashy performance, or by schmoozing and being charming, or by being intimidating. She poses herself as the absentee supervisor, or the "rainmaker," or the invaluable "high-strung genius." She requires frequent vacations, or sabbaticals in which her actual activities are somewhat mysterious. Sustained work, the true key to lasting success—keeping one's nose to the grindstone, tolerating tedium, seeing to the details—is a little too close to responsibility.

Sadly, this same self-limiting factor tends to apply even to sociopaths who are born with special gifts and talents. The kind of intense commitment and daily work required to develop and promote one's art, one's music, or any other creative project is typically impossible for a sociopath. If success can be acquired fortuitously, with only episodic input, then perhaps. But if the art requires a prolonged personal investment, it is lost. In the end, a person without conscience has the same relationship to her own gifts as she does to other people. She does not take care of them.

And sociopathy is almost always a solo routine, another strategy that may sometimes work temporarily but not often in the long run. For the obvious reason of unremitting self-interest, people without conscience make lousy team players. The sociopath is out for himself alone. When he deals with another person, or with a group of people, he attempts to do so by lies, flattery, and the creation of fear. These approaches to success are far weaker and more short-lived than are genuine relating, leadership, and personal involvement, and goals that might have been reached in a partnership, or in a sustained group effort, are usually scuttled by the sociopath's exclusive concern with himself. This path to ultimate failure is typically taken by infamous tyrants, as well as by countless less publicized sociopathic employers, coworkers, and spouses.

When the thrill of manipulating other people takes over, as it does in sociopathy, all other objectives are eclipsed, and the resulting "life disruption," though of a different sort, can be just as severe as the limitations imposed by major depression, chronic anxiety, paranoia, and other mental illnesses. And the emotional bankruptcy of sociopathy means that the sociopath is forever deprived of an authentic emotional intelligence, a capacity for understanding how people work that is an irreplaceable guide for living in the human world. Like Doreen, who actually believes she can increase her personal power by diminishing others, like Skip, who imagines himself permanently immune to society and its rules, like the defeated dictator who is bewildered because the hate-filled mob composed of "his people" will not allow him to negotiate, a person without conscience, even a smart one, tends to be a shortsighted and surprisingly naïve individual who eventually expires of boredom, financial ruin, or a bullet.

Extreme Conscience

Still, the most compelling reason for desiring to have conscience, rather than wishing to be free of it, is not the list of ruinous disadvantages that accrue to sociopathy. No, the best part of possessing a moral sense is the deep and beautiful gift that comes to us inside, and *only* inside, the wrappings of conscience. *The ability to love* comes bundled up in conscience, just as our spirits are bundled up in our bodies. Conscience is the embodiment of love, imbued into our very biology. It lives in the part of the brain that reacts emotionally, and in their favor, when the ones we love need our attention, our help, or even our sacrifice. We have already seen that when someone's mind is not equipped to love, he can have no genuine conscience either, since conscience is an intervening sense of responsibility based in our emotional attachments to others. Now we turn this psychological equation around. The other truth is that should a person have no conscience, he could never truly love. When an imperative sense of responsibility is subtracted from love, all that is left is a thin, tertiary thing—a will to possess, which is not love at all.

Just after September 11, 2001, even as an especially dark and aggressive chapter in our history began, my psychologist friend Bernie told me without hesitation that he would choose conscience over the apparent expediency of being without conscience, but that he could not articulate why. I believe Bernie's intuitive preference was due to the inextricable link between conscience and the ability to love, and that if given the choice between all the power, fame, and money in the world and the privilege of loving his own children, Bernie would choose the latter in a heartbeat. In part, this is because Bernie is a good person. Also, this is because Bernie is a good psychologist, and he knows something about what actually makes people happy.

There is the will to possess and to dominate, and then there is love. Whether or not he could express his reasons at that moment, in choosing conscience, Bernie the psychologist effectively chose love, and this does not surprise me. Dominating can constitute a temporary thrill, but it does not make people happy. Loving does.

But is it not possible to have *too much* conscience? Are there not psychologists who have said that, far from happiness, people can be tyrannized and driven into serious depression by their consciences?

Yes and no. Freud observed that an overactive superego could bully its owner into depression and possibly even suicide. But superego, that yammering disciplinary voice internalized from our early experiences, is not conscience. Neither is something that psychologists call "unhealthy shame," which is not really shame, in the sense of a reaction to having committed bad deeds, so much as it is the irrational belief, instilled by negative messages in childhood, that one's whole self is somehow bad, repellent, worthless. Even a little unhealthy shame is too much, but unhealthy shame is hardly normal conscience, which is an intervening sense of responsibility and not an intrusive feeling of worthlessness and calamity. When contemporary psychologists say that too much conscience is toxic, their vocabulary is careless. They are referring instead to unhealthy shame, or to a strident superego working overtime.

Conscience, our seventh sense, is a different phenomenon altogether. It is a feeling of obligation based in love. So the question lingers: Is extreme conscience debilitating or elevating?

To understand what a great deal of conscience does to the psyche, we can observe the lives and the happiness level of people who have developed their innate sense of conscience into an especially powerful emotional muscle. Each one of us might name different individuals as our moral heroes, from historical or public figures to people we have known personally who have impressed us with their moral commitment. In a systematic study of such people, Anne Colby of Radcliffe's Henry Murray Research Center and William Damon of Brown University's Department of Education made choices of their own. Concerned about what they perceived as our current scarcity of moral leadership, Colby and Damon selected twenty-three individuals whom they considered to be "moral exemplars," eleven men and twelve women whose moral commitment has resulted in signal contributions in many areas, including civil rights and civil liberties, the reduction of poverty and hunger, religious freedom, environmental protection, and peace. These twenty-three people are diverse in terms of race, religion, socioeconomic status, and specific goals, but all have one thing in common: an extraordinarily powerful sense of conscience, an "overdeveloped" sense that they are responsible for the welfare of their fellow human beings. They represent, from a psychologist's vantage point, the diametric emotional and mental opposite of the sociopaths we have been discussing.

Colby and Damon's "moral exemplars" include Virginia Foster Durr, the Southern belle turned civil rights activist who was the first person to hug Rosa Parks when she stepped out of jail; Suzie Valadez, who has spent many years feeding, clothing, and providing medical care to thousands of poor Mexicans in Ciudad Juárez; Jack Coleman, a former president of Haverford College, noted for his "blue-collar sabbaticals" as a ditch digger, a garbageman, a homeless person; businessman Cabell Brand, who devoted himself to the creation of Total Action Against Poverty in Roanoke, Virginia; and Charleszetta Waddles, founder of the Perpetual Mission, who dedicated her life to helping the elderly and the poor, the unwed mothers, the prostitutes, and the abused children of Detroit, Michigan.

The researchers studied autobiographies and oral histories and conducted in-depth interviews with each of the twenty-three exemplars and their coworkers. In a book that documents their findings, entitled *Some Do Care: Contemporary Lives of Moral Commitment,* they report three striking commonalities among individuals of extreme conscience. The authors label these shared characteristics as (1) "certainty," (2) "positivity," and (3) "unity of self and moral goals." "Certainty" refers to an exceptional clarity concerning what the exemplars believe to be right, and also their sense of an unequivocal personal responsibility to act on those beliefs. "Positivity" expresses the exemplars' affirmative approach to life, their extraordinary enjoyment of their work, and their marked optimism, often despite hardship or even danger. And "unity of self and moral goals" describes the integration of the subjects' moral stance with their conception of their own identity, and the perceived sameness of their moral and personal goals.

"Unity" means that, for such people, conscience is not just a guiding light. It is *who they are.* In an attempt to describe his sense of personal identity, one of the exemplars, Cabell Brand, explained in an interview, "Who I am is what I'm able to do and how I feel all the time—each day, each moment. . . . It's hard for me to separate who I am from what I want to do and what I am doing."

Colby and Damon consider this third characteristic, the "unity of self and moral goals," to be their most important finding, and crucially important to the understanding of conscience and its effects. When conscience grows sufficiently strong, apparently it unifies the human psyche in a unique and beneficial way, and rather than causing "life disruption," extreme conscience significantly enhances life satisfaction. Colby and Damon write, "Our exemplars have been invulnerable to the debilitating effects of privation because all they have needed for personal success is the productive pursuit of their moral mission." In unself-conscious defiance of our cultural tendency to set conscience and self-interest in opposition to each other, Colby and Damon's exemplars "defined their own welfare and self-interest in moral terms and were, with very few exceptions, extremely happy and fulfilled." Far from causing them suffering, or making them into dupes, their exceptional sense of obligation to other people made them happy.

Conscience, our sense of responsibility toward one another, allows us to live together, in our homes and on our planet. It helps to create meaning in our lives, and stands between us and an empty existence of meaningless competitions. A very large sense of conscience can integrate moral intention, personal desire, and identity in the mind—right action becomes *who we are*—and for this reason, extreme conscience appears to be a rare exact-fit key to human happiness.

So here is my best psychological advice: As you look around our world and try to figure out what is going on and who is "winning," do not wish to have less conscience. Wish for more.

Celebrate your fate.

Having a conscience, you may never be able to do exactly as you please, or just what you would need to do in order to succeed easily or ultimately in the material world. And so perhaps you will never wield great financial or political power over other people. Maybe you will never command the respect of the masses, or their fear. On the contrary, you may suffer painful bouts of conscience that cause you to act quite against your own self-serving ambitions. And you may have to work hard all your life, giving up the temptations of childlike dependency, because you want your own children to thrive. You may yourself be caught up in the snares of sociopaths from time to time, and on account of your scruples, you may never be able to take satisfactory revenge on the people who have hurt you. And, yes, you may never become the dictator of a small country.

But you will be able to look at your children asleep in their beds and feel that unbearable surge of awe and thanksgiving. You will be able to keep others alive in your heart long after they are gone. You will have genuine friends. Unlike the hollow, risk-pursuing few who are deprived of a seventh sense, you will go through your life fully aware of the warm and comforting, infuriating, confusing, compelling, and sometimes joyful presence of other human beings, and along with your conscience you will be given the chance to take the largest risk of all, which, as we all know, is to love.

Conscience truly is Mother Nature's better bargain. Its value is evident on a grand historic scale, and as we will see in the next chapter, it is precious to us even in our ordinary day-to-day dealings with friends and neighbors. Along with an entire neighborhood, let us now try to spend a day with an unfortunate and sociopathic woman named Tillie. From Tillie, we can learn—though she never will—that conscience makes everyday experience worth having.

ELEVEN

groundhog day

What is not good for the swarm is not good for the bee.

—*Marcus Aurelius*

Tillie is someone personality theorist Theodore Millon would call an "abrasive psychopath." She is sociopathic but, regrettably for Tillie, she lacks the sociopath's customary charm and finesse. Instead, to use Millon's words, she "acts in an overtly and directly contentious and quarrelsome way," and "everything and everyone is an object available for nagging and assaulting." Tillie's specific talent is to take the smallest, subtlest whisper of conflict and amplify it into a shouting match. She excels at the creation of hostility and bitterness where there was none before, and specializes in provoking people who ordinarily are gentle and peace-loving.

In Tillie's universe, Tillie is always right, and she takes self-righteous pleasure in opposing and frustrating her opponents, who are seemingly everywhere and somehow always wrong. Her mission in life is to correct the world, a calling she heeds without hesitation or conscience. In this mission, she perceives that she is unappreciated by others, which further justifies her behavior toward them.

This morning, Tillie has discovered a groundhog in her backyard. As she watches from her sunroom, it sits back on its round haunches in the grass and turns its alert little face in every direction, as if surveying Tillie's property. When Tillie opens the sliding door to get a better look, the animal freezes in place for a moment, then waddles away and vanishes into the ground at the edge of the lawn, at a point where Tillie's yard meets that of her neighbors Catherine and Fred.

Tillie makes a mental note of where its hole must be, then goes out to stand on her deck, a white-haired woman of seventy in a blue-checkered housedress, appearing for all the world to be the archetypal kind and wise old woman. As she gazes with interest across the lawn, anyone looking on might remark that her demeanor and bottom-heavy shape are not altogether different from the groundhog's.

Tillie's neighbors on the other side of her house and up the hill, Greta and Jerry, also happen to be having breakfast in their sunroom and can see Tillie there on her deck. They are too far away to notice the groundhog. All they can make out is seventy-year-old Tillie, standing very still in her blue-and-white dress.

Thirty-five-year-old Greta, the manager of a local department store, says to her husband, Jerry, a building contractor, "Damn, I wish that awful woman would just move away. How long has she been here now?"

"Fifteen months," replies Jerry.

Greta smiles mirthlessly. "But who's counting, right? I know I shouldn't wish people gone, but she's just so incredibly *mean.* And controlling. I don't know how she can even stand her own self."

Jerry sighs and says, "Maybe we could buy her out."

Greta is about to laugh, and then she realizes that Jerry is not joking. All of a sudden, she understands that her normally even-tempered husband despises Tillie every bit as much as she does. She feels chilly, and a little guilty, and goes back into the kitchen to get some more hot coffee.

When she comes back, Jerry is still staring at the old woman on her deck. He says, "No, we really can't afford to buy her out. Maybe she'll just move. Seems like you'd move if everybody in the neighborhood hated you as much as everybody hates her."

Greta points out, "Well, the thing is, I bet she gets this reaction wherever she goes."

"Yeah, probably. Where was she living before?"

"Don't know," answers Greta. Then, beginning to feel somewhat gratified that Jerry shares her sentiments, she says, "Do you believe this? It was last week, I think, she called me and said we shouldn't have any more fires in our fireplace. She's 'allergic to wood smoke,' don't you know?"

"*What?* You never told me she did that! That's crazy!" Jerry clenches his fists, and then changes his assessment. "No, that's not crazy. That's just horse crap. We'll have a fire in the damn fireplace tonight. In fact, I'll bring in some more wood before I leave for work."

"But it's supposed to get really warm today."

"Who cares?"

This time, Greta does laugh. "Do you know how we sound?"

Jerry looks at his wife sheepishly, and the corners of his mouth begin to turn up. He unclenches his fists and cracks his knuckles a couple of times to get rid of the tension.

Greta and Jerry's neighbor across the street and down three houses is an elderly widow named Sunny. At this very moment, though she cannot actually see Tillie on her back deck like Greta and Jerry can, Sunny too is thinking about how mean Tillie is. Yesterday, Tillie called the police because Sunny had parked her car on the street in front of her own house. Sunny has always parked her car in that big space between the street and her house, since her husband passed away ten years ago, because she is afraid to back out of her driveway into the traffic. The young policeman came and made her put it in the driveway. He apologized several times, but still he said

Tillie was right. It was a violation. Sunny has not even had breakfast yet, and already she is dreading her trip to the grocery store today, because she will have to back her car out alone. She feels like crying. And that car was nowhere near Tillie's house!

As Sunny laments across the street, Tillie, on her backyard deck, decides that the groundhog is not going to reappear right now. She goes back into her house, where she can no longer be seen by the breakfasting Greta and Jerry up the hill. While Greta and Jerry drink the rest of their coffee and try to talk about something else, Tillie, in her kitchen, picks up the phone and calls Catherine, the next-door neighbor with whom she now shares a groundhog.

Catherine teaches the sixth grade. She has taught school since she was twenty-two, and now her sixtieth birthday is coming. She thinks she ought to retire, but the notion only makes her sad. Her teaching, her kids, mean the world to her, and she really does not want to stop working. Her husband, Fred, who is seven years older and already retired, understands this and is patient with her.

"Whenever you're ready," he always says. "I like to putter around the house and fix things anyway." And then they both laugh. Fred can barely replace burned-out lightbulbs. Until he reluctantly gave up the mantle a year ago, he was the editor of their regional newspaper. He is a good, quiet, bookish man who loved his work, too, and still contributes an "emeritus" human-interest column called "People You Should Know."

When the phone rings, Fred is reading in the living room, and Catherine is in the kitchen, getting ready to go to work early. The trill of the phone at such an hour makes Catherine jump. She answers it quickly.

"Hello?"

"Catherine," says Tillie abruptly, snipping the word as if she were angry.

"Yes, this is Catherine. Tillie? Tillie, my goodness, it's seven in the morning. Are you all right?"

"Yes. I'm fine. I just saw a groundhog in the yard, and I thought you'd like to know."

"A what? A groundhog?"

"Yes, in the back, between our properties."

"Well, that's . . . interesting. Must have been cute, I guess. Was it?"

"I suppose. Anyway, I know you're busy. I just thought you should know about the animal. We can talk about it later. Good-bye."

"Uh, right. Talk later. Well, good-bye then, Tillie."

Catherine hangs up the phone, baffled, and Fred calls to her, "What was that?"

She walks into the living room, where he sits with his book, and answers, "That was Tillie."

"Oh," says Fred, rolling his eyes. "What did she want?"

"She wanted to tell me she saw a groundhog in the backyard."

"Why did she want to tell you that?"

Catherine shakes her head slowly and says, "I don't have the slightest idea."

"Ah Tillie!" pronounces Fred, raising his right arm above his head in mock salute.

As she finishes her morning routine, Catherine feels confused and slightly ill at ease, knowing that with Tillie there is always a thickening plot, and that the denouement is likely to be controlling and upsetting. But for the life of her, she cannot imagine what this thing with the groundhog is about. Does Tillie want to have it removed? Is Tillie asking her permission in some roundabout way? Also, Catherine and Fred have lived in this same house for thirty years, and they have never once seen a groundhog in the yard. How odd.

As she is about to leave for school, the phone rings a second time. She thinks it must be Tillie again, but instead it is another neighbor, sweet, soft-spoken Sunny, and she is in tears. Sunny tells Catherine that Tillie has made her park her car in the driveway, and now she is trapped. Can someone help? Can Catherine and Fred take her to the store today? Learning about this newest exploit of Tillie's, Catherine feels the blood rushing angrily to her face, but in her calmest voice, she reassures Sunny that of course Fred will drive her to the store. How about lunchtime? Also, Fred knows the chief of police very well, and maybe something can be done about the problem with Sunny's parking space.

Teaching her class of sixth graders all day, Catherine forgets about Tillie, but when she gets home at about 4:30, she remembers the early-morning phone call and begins to feel uneasy all over again. She was planning to take a nap before dinner, but as she sits down on the bed, her uneasiness gets suddenly stronger, and she is drawn to the window. The bedroom is on the second floor, and from here, Catherine has a clear view of the whole backyard, and Tillie's as well. The day has been unseasonably warm, and all those nice forsythias Fred planted at the back edge of their yard are beginning to bloom. There is the wide back lawn, and beyond that the long row of little yellow forsythia blossoms, and then the gray-brown shadow of the still-leafless conservation forest that borders all the backyards on this side of the street.

And also, rather strangely, there is Tillie, standing right in the middle of her lawn. She is still wearing her checkered blue-and-white dress and has added a wide-brimmed straw hat, as if she were about to do some ladylike gardening.

But Tillie never gardens.

As Catherine watches from her bedroom window, Tillie looks around the yard, seems to spy something she wants, and marches over to it. She bends and, with obvious effort, lifts an object from the ground that looks to Catherine like a large white rock, about the size and shape of a small watermelon. Studying the scene more intently, Catherine realizes that the object is indeed a rock, a small boulder really, and nearly too much for Tillie to hold. But Tillie embraces the rock with both arms, stooping in a way that is painful to watch, and begins to waddle unsteadily in the direction of Fred's forsythia plants.

A phrase from the morning's phone conversation echoes in Catherine's head—"in the back, between our properties"—and in this same moment, Catherine knows exactly what Tillie is doing. The groundhog's burrow! Tillie is going to use that rock to plug up the den of the groundhog she told her about.

Catherine is appalled. She feels light-headed and sick, almost as if she were witnessing a murder. She needs to do something, but going out and confronting Tillie directly would be like arguing with a rabid wolverine. In truth, though Catherine does not like to admit this to herself, Tillie frightens her in general, for reasons she cannot even put into words. Why should a rather insignificant seventy-year-old woman frighten her?

And how did Tillie know she would be watching from the house right now? *Did* she know?

Catherine begins to pace across the bedroom, from the window to the old oak dresser and back to the window. She sees Tillie drop the rock clumsily onto a spot just beyond the forsythias, midway between two small willows at the edge of the woods, and she marks the location carefully in her mind. Then she paces back to the dresser and stares at herself in the antique mirror. While Tillie swipes at loose dirt on the front of her dress and parades back across the lawn to her deck, Catherine continues to stare into her own eyes in the mirror. That poor little animal, she keeps thinking. What if he's trapped?

Finally, Catherine knows what she wants to do. And she must tell Fred. He can help.

Fred has been at the newspaper, visiting with some of his old friends. When he comes home, Catherine tells him what Tillie has done. He says, "Well, I guess in this case Tillie got two with one stone, literally."

"What do you mean?"

"You and the little woodchuck, both."

"Oh, right. That's really true, isn't it?" says Catherine glumly.

"It would appear so. Sure you don't want me to go over there and have it out with her?"

"No. She'd just do it again. I want to help the groundhog, so he'll be okay. Go with me?"

"Do I have a choice?"

Catherine smiles and hugs him. "Not really," she says.

They make dinner together, as is their habit, and wait until about nine o'clock, when it is completely dark outside. Fred suggests flashlights, but Catherine thinks Tillie would see them.

"She'll know we liberated him, and she'll just cover him again tomorrow."

"We'll have to take at least one, to find the burrow once we get there."

"Yes. Right. Okay, maybe a penlight? For when we get there."

They set out across the yard at a snail's pace, so as not to trip in the darkness. Fred takes the lead, and Catherine follows, arms held out in front of her like a sleepwalker's, to keep her balance. When they get to the far end of the lawn, they follow along the row of forsythia bushes until there are no more forsythias. Then, in wonder, like a child, Catherine takes a step into the even more complete darkness beyond, hoping that her hands, and not her face, will find one of the willows.

She feels a branch, takes a deep breath, and whispers, "Okay, Fred. Penlight."

Fred takes the light out of his pocket, holds it close to the ground, and turns it on. After a few moments, they find the melon-size rock, somewhat more easily than they could have hoped, because the rock is smooth and white and the surrounding earth is dark. Catherine exhales and pushes a loose strand of hair behind her left ear. She and Fred bend down and lift the rock together, revealing a surprisingly small hole in the ground, considering it is used by a fat little groundhog.

Catherine has an impulse to shine the penlight into the hole to check on its occupant. But then she realizes that she will not see much, and that she may scare the animal.

Arm in arm, whispering and containing their laughter, she and Fred stumble home.

Tillie does not see them. As they return from their mission, she has already been drinking and sulking for several hours, as usual. She sits on a sofa in her living room and pours herself glasses of Glenlivet, trying to drown out the monotony of her life and the idiots she continually has to deal with. The only thing that makes this evening different from any other is the accumulation of packing boxes now stacked around her.

Inside her drunken fog, she congratulates herself on her brilliant idea not to put up a FOR SALE sign this time. She thinks, I'll take these cretins by surprise. Their stupid mouths will gape.

The good-for-nothing real estate agent keeps telling her that not using a sign is shooting herself in the foot, and that he really thinks she should wait for a higher offer. This buyer came in under her price. But Tillie cannot wait. She has never liked waiting. She will have her moment, and her moment will be tomorrow morning. And then everyone in this whole horrible neighborhood will be in complete shock about her move. She is sure of it. The agent does not understand why secrecy matters, but he is a fool, so why listen to him? She has taken losses before when she wanted to get out of a house fast. It's all in the game, she thinks to herself. All in the game. You can't stay in a place where the people won't listen to you. And giving them a parting shot is extremely important.

Tillie has a trust fund from her deceased father that has supported her for most of her life. These days, she says she is "retired," but she never really worked. She used to paint watercolors sometimes when she was younger, but she never sold any of them. She would like to purchase grander houses, but her wretched mother keeps hanging on, and so she cannot get her hands on the rest of the money. Her mother is nearly a hundred years old, and still she has not died. Tillie is stuck in these dreadful middle-class neighborhoods, knowing that, by rights, she should have a wealthier lifestyle. She visits her mother periodically, because she certainly does not want to be written out of the will, and the bedridden old woman always reminds her of a half-plucked parakeet squawking in a cage. What she has to say is just about that interesting.

Nothing is very interesting, really. Suffocating the rodent was okay for a few minutes, and she hopes Catherine was watching. Catherine would have a stroke. But then that project was over, and there was nothing else to do. She cannot imagine what these absurd people on all sides of her do that seems to occupy them so completely as they scurry about their little lives. They must have brains the size of peas.

She pours herself another drink and consumes it in one gulp. Not yet packed into a box, a painting that she made when she was still in her twenties hangs over the unused fireplace, so faded that the image can hardly be made out in the shadows of the ill-lighted living room. Hunched on the sofa, she looks up at it and dimly recalls the beach scene she stood in all those decades ago. Then all she sees are the pinpoints of stars before her eyes that she waits for most nights of her life, just before she blacks out.

The next morning is Saturday, a bit cooler than yesterday, and not a cloud in the sky.

Across the street and down a few houses, Sunny opens the lace curtains in her front window, and as the sun streams in, she takes in the happy view of her car parked where it is supposed to be—on the street. And there it will stay parked. Fred talked to the police chief yesterday after lunch, and got everything all squared away for her. "*Freedom,*" she breathes to herself. She tries to think what she can do for Fred and Catherine. Maybe she can bake them something. Imagining how much they will like that, she feels even more cheerful.

In the house up the hill, Greta has the weekend off, and she and Jerry sleep late. When they slowly rouse themselves and go out to the sunroom to drink their coffee, they notice a big moving truck in Tillie's driveway.

"Does that mean what I think it means?" Jerry asks, staring at the truck. "Or are we still in bed, dreaming?"

"Got to be dreaming," says Greta, also staring. "I never saw a sign. Did you ever see a sign over there?"

"Nope."

Just now, two men wearing canvas coveralls come out of Tillie's house, each carrying one end of a sofa. Greta and Jerry look at each other and begin to laugh. Jerry laughs so hard, he spills some of his coffee.

Greta asks him, "Why do you suppose she kept it a secret?"

"Why does she do anything? But it doesn't matter anymore, does it? Unbelievable."

Greta is thoughtful for a moment, and then says, "How old do you suppose she is?"

"I don't know. Not young."

"I wonder whether she ever had any children. Oh wow. Can you imagine being one of her *children*?"

"Worse yet, can you imagine being *her*?"

"So, do you think we should feel sorry for her?" Greta asks.

Jerry grins and waves his hand dismissively at the furniture-moving scene in the distance. "Well, I'm not sure, sweetheart. But if we're going to feel sorry for her, let's do it over breakfast, okay? Remember that strudel?"

"Yes!" says Greta, smacking her lips. She picks up both coffee mugs, and they abandon the view from the sunroom in favor of the pastry in the kitchen.

Since they are in the house next door to Tillie's, Catherine and Fred also notice the activities of the men from the moving truck, and wonder why they never saw a FOR SALE sign or heard from Tillie that she was moving. Fred rolls his eyes again, and Catherine shakes her head. But then they are distracted by another phone call, this one from their daughter and son-in-law, who say that in two weeks they and four-year-old Katie are flying out for another visit. Catherine is beside herself with excitement, and Tillie's moving day, still in progress outside, is forgotten.

Two hours later, when the truck pulls away from Tillie's house, no one is watching. All is quiet again.

In Catherine and Fred's backyard, by the forsythias at the far opposite end of the row, the groundhog clambers out of his second hole and stands up as tall as he can on his short hind legs. His black eyes glinting in the bright sunlight, he peers over at a big white rock lying near his first hole, at the other end of the yellow bushes. Then he gazes up toward Tillie's empty house. Finally, his attention settles on a patch of dandelions growing in the soft earth just in front of him. Another groundhog, slightly smaller, wiggles out of the hole. They sit down groundhog-fashion, share a leisurely luncheon of new stems, and amble off into the woods.

TWELVE

conscience in its purest form: science votes for morality

He is not a perfect Muslim who eats his fill and lets his neighbor go hungry.

—*Muhammad*

For what shall it profit a man, if he shall gain the whole world, and lose his own soul?

—*Jesus*

The man who knows how to split the atom but has no love in his heart becomes a monster.

—*Krishnamurti*

One way or another, a life without conscience is a failed life. Those of us who love and have conscience are really very lucky, even as we go about our everyday lives of work, reflexive give-and-take, and ordinary pleasures.

And usually conscience is just that: reflexive and ordinary. Without fanfare and mostly without being noticed, conscience grants little bits of meaning to our normal and spontaneous day-to-day interactions with everyone and everything around us. Catherine and Fred were not thinking about high-minded principles when they set out to liberate the groundhog, which, as it turns out, was not trapped in the first place. They were not being pious or courageous, not particularly effective, and certainly not rational. It was simply that trying to help the animal seemed right and somehow made them *feel good.* Moving that rock was, to use an old and universally understood expression, "good for their souls."

Where conscience is concerned, over the centuries Western culture has progressed from faith in an immutable God-sent knowledge of right and wrong to a belief in Freud's concept of a punitive superego to an understanding that conscience is based in our normal and positive relatedness to one another. As an intervening sense of responsibility seated in our emotional attachments, conscience has evolved into a purely psychological construct. But, in a kind of philosophical full circle back to its beginnings in the church, conscience is also the place where psychology and spirituality meet, an issue on which the recommendations of psychology and the teachings of the major religious and spiritual traditions of the world completely concur. In a remarkable confluence—even the radical materialists and the mystics in a tacit meeting of the minds—behavioral science, evolutionary psychology, and all traditional theologies agree that having a strong conscience is extremely advantageous, and that not having one at all most commonly leads to disaster, for groups and also for individuals.

A psychologist would say that when we take some responsibility for the welfare of others, our actions feel natural (or "ego-syntonic") and our own life satisfaction is enhanced. The Bible says simply, "It is more blessed to give than to receive." As a psychologist, I can tell you that the absence of an intervening sense of responsibility based in emotional attachment is associated with an endless, usually futile preoccupation with domination, and results in substantial life disruption and eventual deterioration. Buddha put it this way: "All that we are is the result of what we have thought. If a man speaks or acts with an evil thought, pain follows him. If a man speaks or acts with a pure thought, happiness follows him, like a shadow that never leaves him."

In their psychological study of individuals with exceptional conscience, Anne Colby and William Damon write, "A positivity that includes optimism, love, and joy is . . . closely linked with morality, as we see in the lives of our exemplars." Buddha again agrees. He says, "To walk safely through the maze of human life, one needs the light of wisdom and the guidance of virtue."

And, of course, there is the Golden Rule, which is humankind's most ancient ethic of reciprocity, and perhaps the most succinct and clearly operationalized moral philosophy ever conceived. Confucius was merely recording an even older Chinese saying when he wrote, "Do not do to others what you would not want done to you," and when Jesus said, "Do unto others as you would have them do unto you," he was referring to an already time-honored Jewish proverb that instructed, "What is hateful to you, do not to your fellow man. This is the law: all the rest is commentary." The Mahabharata tells followers of Hinduism, "This is the sum of the Dharma: Do naught unto others which would cause you pain if done to you." And in indigenous traditions as well—the Yoruba of Nigeria say, "One going to take a pointed stick to pinch a baby bird should first try it on himself to feel how it hurts." And the Lakota religious leader Black Elk taught, "All things are our relatives; what we do to everything, we do to ourselves. All is really One."

The smattering of religions that do not adhere to moral reciprocity are contemporary, and tend to make the moral warmth of the ancient Golden Rule seem even more attractive by their own blood-chilling nature. As an illustration, one can cite the Creativity Movement, a militantly anti-Semitic and anti-Christian group formerly called the World Church of the Creator, which is a religion founded on the love of the "White Race" and the prescribed hatred of everyone else. Within this doctrine, everyone who is not "White" is by definition a member of one of the "mud races." The central moral precept of the Creativity Movement is expressed as follows: "What is good for the White Race is the highest virtue; what is bad for the White Race is the ultimate sin." Unsurprisingly, the long-term goal of the Creativity Movement is to organize the "White Race" to achieve world domination.

In welcome contrast, most religions and spiritual traditions subscribe to the Golden Rule, and also to some form of Black Elk's belief that "All is really One." Oneness is a more fundamental tenet for some religions than others. For example, while the Judeo-Christian tradition instructs its followers to love their neighbors, Eastern mysticism teaches that individuality, the ego, is an illusion to begin with, that we are not distinct from God or from one another, and therefore, in a spiritual sense, we *are* our neighbors. In *Peace Is Every Step,* Vietnamese Buddhist master Thich Nhat Hanh tries to explain this aspect of Eastern thought for Westerners by telling us that we "inter-are." We are ineluctably and inextricably bound up with everyone and everything in the universe, and this state of interbeing is the reason we should not selfishly (and vainly) chase our goals of individual acquisition and power.

Though less conspicuously, a belief in oneness is part of the Judeo-Christian tradition as well. In 1939, as yet another shattering attempt at world domination rumbled in Europe, Jewish theologian and philosopher Martin Buber addressed the National Conference of Palestinian Teachers in Tel Aviv. He concluded his address by saying, "Nothing remains but what rises above the abyss of today's monstrous problems, as above every abyss of every time: the wing-beat of the spirit and the creative word. But he who can see and hear out of unity will also behold and discern again what can be beheld and discerned eternally. The educator who helps to bring man back to his own unity will help to put him again face to face with God."

In whatever tradition they occur, spiritual practices focused on an awareness of interbeing tend to have the intriguing psychological side effect of bringing significant earthly happiness to their most devoted practitioners, almost regardless of external circumstances. In a book that is a collaboration between psychologist Daniel Goleman and His Holiness the Dalai Lama, entitled *Destructive Emotions: A Scientific Dialogue with the Dalai Lama,* Goleman writes, "The very act of concern for others' well-being, it seems, creates a greater state of well-being within oneself." In recent years, increasing numbers of scientists have echoed this impression. At a 2002 conference on science and the mind, attended by the Dalai Lama, distinguished Australian neurobiologist Jack Pettigrew remarked, "If you go to Dharamsala [Indian home of the Tibetan community in exile], you go up through the fog in midwinter and you come out in the bright sunshine, it's like going to heaven. What strikes you immediately is the happy, smiling faces of the Tibetans, who don't have much, have been terribly deprived, and yet they are happy. Well, why are they happy?"

The Dalai Lama himself is interested in answering this question scientifically, and in finding a secular way to create the compassionate sense of interbeing that is achieved by devout practitioners of Tibetan Buddhist meditation. To this end, he has launched an international series of dialogues between scientists and Buddhist scholars, the most recent of which, in 2003, was cosponsored by the Mind and Life Institute in Colorado and the McGovern Institute of the Massachusetts Institute of Technology. He intends these dialogues to yield practical solutions to the destructive states of mind that both the Buddhists and the scientists view as the root of human conflict and suffering.

As a psychologist, I am particularly taken with the Dalai Lama's description of those whom I might refer to as sociopaths, or as people devoid of an intervening sense of obligation based in connectedness to others. He refers to such individuals as "people who don't have well-developed human lives." More specifically, the Dalai Lama said of the World Trade Center attacks, "Technology is a good thing, but the use of technology in the hands of people who don't have well-developed human lives can be disastrous."

To the extent that a person's capacity to have a well-developed human life is facilitated or limited by his or her particular gray matter, this Buddhist conception of sociopathy highlights what is one of the most interesting confluences of all, that between religion and neuropsychology. Perhaps sociopathy is a life lesson that is taught not by some physical facility or limitation, but by an emotional debility. In other words, some people must learn what it is like to live with extreme beauty, or no legs, or as a beggar, and others, those with no conscience, must learn what it means to live without being able to care about others. There is an irony here, in that this karmic state, if you will, may indeed be a reason to find sociopaths pitiable, as we might pity blind orphans, whether or not we believe in the devices of karma.

Though psychology recognizes the value of compassion and of sensing oneness, psychologists have so far not researched any direct methods to achieve these, thus leaving sociopaths and especially our healthier disciples somewhat in the lurch where the heightening of conscience is concerned. As ways to increase life satisfaction, psychologists increasingly recommend moral education for normal children and giving and volunteerism for adults, but psychologists have traditionally been much more interested in endeavors such as "strengthening interpersonal boundaries" and "assertiveness training." In this regard, psychology relative to spirituality reminds me of the hungry traveler in an ancient parable from India called "The Wise Woman's Stone." A version of this parable, the author of which is long lost to antiquity, can be found in a collection of stories compiled by Arthur Lenehan, published in 1994 by, ironically, The Economics Press:

> A wise woman who was traveling in the mountains found a precious stone in a stream. The next day she met another traveler

> who was hungry, and the wise woman opened her bag to share her food. The hungry traveler saw the precious stone and asked the woman to give it to him. She did so without hesitation.
>
> The traveler left, rejoicing in his good fortune. He knew the stone was worth enough to give him security for a lifetime. But a few days later he came back to return the stone to the wise woman.
>
> "I've been thinking," he said, "I know how valuable the stone is, but I give it back in the hope that you can give me something even more precious. Give me what you have within you that enabled you to give me the stone."

The wise and happy Tibetan Buddhists, and certainly the Dalai Lama himself, are reminiscent of Colby and Damon's exemplars of extreme conscience, such as Suzie Valadez, who feeds the poor in Mexico, and former college president Jack Coleman, who tried to foster his own sense of interbeing and compassion by being a ditch digger, a garbage collector, a homeless person. Both the Buddhist monks and the psychological exemplars illustrate that the awareness provided by extreme conscience improves people's lives and makes them happy. This happiness is not the product of any cognitive strategy or reattribution of temporary failures to the cosmos and long-term successes to oneself. In fact, Colby and Damon report that most of their moral exemplars are insistent realists regarding the circumstances of human life and their own limited potential to alter these conditions. No, rather than mere cognitive adaptation, exceptional conscience involves the strong and steadying sensation of being part of something greater than oneself.

Indeed, conscience would seem to be the nexus of psychology and spirituality, as revealed by what psychologists now know about the singularly uplifting effects of a moral sense based in emotional connectedness. In religion and spirituality, the experience at this locus is called by names such as oneness, unity, interbeing. In psychology, it is called conscience or the moral sense. Whatever its name, it is a powerful integrator of human thought, emotion, and action that knew its origins in our primeval biological past. Through our genes, our brains, and perhaps our very souls, it has become a protective, productive, and mood-sustaining force in our psychological and social lives, and for thousands of years has spoken to our most transcendent traditions and to the most admirable members of our race. Conscience is the still small voice that has been trying since the infancy of our species to tell us that we are evolutionarily, emotionally, and spiritually One, and that if we seek peace and happiness, we must behave that way.

Conscience, and uniquely conscience, can compel us out of our own skins and into the skin of another, or even into contact with the Absolute. It is based in our emotional ties to one another. In its purest form, it is called love. And wonderfully, both mystics and evolutionary psychologists, who concur on not much else, agree that people by their normal nature are more likely to be loving than malevolent. This conclusion signifies a breathtaking departure from our usual, more cynical view of ourselves.

Theologians and scientists agree also that the human mistakes tending to contravene our normally benevolent nature are twofold. The first mistake is the desire to be personally in control of others and of the world. This motivation involves the illusion that domination is a worthwhile goal, an illusion that is most fixed in the sociopathic mind. And the second tragic error is moral exclusion. We know there to be endless danger in deciding that the "other" is something less than human—the other gender, the other race, the foreigner, the "enemy," and perhaps even the sociopath himself—which is why the question of what to do with the moral outlaw is such an uneasy one in theology and also in psychology. How do we face the potentially cataclysmic challenge of people who simply "don't have well-developed human lives"? So far, psychology has left this question completely unanswered, though it would seem an ever more pressing issue as time goes by and technology is proliferated. After all, the devil is evolving, too.

As for the question of who is more fortunate, the person ruthlessly engaged only in exactly what he wants to do, or you, who are obligated by your conscience—once again, I ask you to imagine what you would be like if you had no seventh sense. But this time as you envision your huge influence and wealth, or your permanent leisure without guilt, imagine it while bearing in mind what conscience and only conscience can bring to a life, what it *has* brought to yours. Picture clearly the face of someone you love more than all of your earthly possessions, someone for whom you would run headlong into a burning building if this were required of you—a parent, a brother, a sister, a dear friend, your life partner, your child. Try to picture that same face—a parent's, or a daughter's, or a son's—weeping in grief, or smiling in peace and joy.

And now imagine for a moment that you could look forever and feel absolutely nothing, no love, no desire to help or even to smile back.

But do not imagine this careening emptiness too long, though it would stretch throughout a lifetime if you were a person without conscience, someone who could guiltlessly do anything at all. Rather, return to your feelings. In your mind, see the face you love, touch a cheek, hear the laughter.

Conscience blesses our individual lives with just this kind of meaning every day. Without it, we would be emotionally hollow and bored, and would spend our days pursuing repetitive games of our own misguided creation.

For most of us, most of the time, conscience is so ordinary, so daily, and so spontaneous that we do not even notice it. But conscience is also much larger than we are. It is one side of a confrontation between an ancient faction of amoral self-interest that has always been doomed, both psychologically and spiritually, and a circle of moral minds just as ageless. As a psychologist and as a citizen of the species, I vote for the people with conscience, for the ones who are loving and committed, for the generous and gentle souls. I am most impressed by those individuals who feel, quite simply, that hurting others is wrong and that kindness is right, and whose actions are quietly directed by this moral sense every day of their lives. They are an elite of their own. They are old and young. They are people who have been gone for hundreds of years and the baby who will be born tomorrow. They come from every nation, culture, and religion. They are the most aware and focused members of our species. And they are, and always have been, our hope.

notes

Introduction: Imagine

page 6 *now thought to be present in about 4 percent of the population:* See K. Barry et al., "Conduct Disorder and Antisocial Personality in Adult Primary Care Patients," *Journal of Family Practice* 45 (1997): 151–158; R. Bland, S. Newman, and H. Orn, "Lifetime Prevalence of Psychiatric Disorders in Edmonton," *Acta Psychiatrica Scandinavica* 77 (1988): 24–32; J. Samuels et al., "DSM-III Personality Disorders in the Community," *American Journal of Psychiatry* 151 (1994): 1055–1062; and U.S. Department of Health and Human Services, *Substance Abuse and Mental Health Statistical Sourcebook* (Rockville, MD: Substance Abuse and Mental Health Services Administration, 1991).

page 6 *This condition of missing conscience:* For the past two hundred years, sociopathy, variously conceptualized, has been called by a variety of different names in the Western world. For a detailed discussion of the history of such labels and diagnoses, see T. Millon, E. Simonsen, and M. Birket-Smith, "Historical Conceptions of Psychopathy in the United States and Europe," in *Psychopathy: Antisocial, Criminal, and Violent Behavior*, eds. T. Millon et al. (New York: Guilford Press, 1998).

page 6 *According to the current bible of psychiatric labels:* American Psychiatric Association, *Diagnostic and Statistical Manual of Mental Disorders*, 4th ed. (Washington, D.C.: American Psychiatric Association, 1994). For detailed descriptions and critiques of the APA field trials used to evaluate the current diagnostic criteria for antisocial personality disorder, see W. Livesley, ed., *The DSM-IV Personality Disorders* (New York: Guilford Press, 1995).

page 6 *Other researchers and clinicians:* See, for example, R. Hare, "Psychopathy: A Clinical Construct Whose Time Has Come," *Criminal Justice and Behavior* 23 (1996): 25–54.

page 7 *And sociopaths are noted especially:* The accepted expression is "shallowness of emotion," although in the case of sociopathy, a more accurate description would be "absence of emotion."

page 8 *As I have detailed in case studies:* M. Stout, *The Myth of Sanity: Divided Consciousness and the Promise of Awareness* (New York: Viking Penguin, 2001).

page 12 *Robert Hare:* R. Hare et al., "The Revised Psychopathy Checklist: Descriptive Statistics, Reliability, and Factor Structure," *Psychological Assessment* 2 (1990): 338–341.

page 12 *Of his subjects, Hare:* R. Hare, *Without Conscience: The Disturbing World of the Psychopaths Among Us* (New York: Guilford Press, 1999), p. 207.

page 12 *And Hervey Cleckley:* H. Cleckley, *The Mask of Sanity*, 5th ed. (St. Louis, MO: Mosby, 1976), p. 90.

page 13 *with its known relationship to behaviors:* For a review of research on problems associated with sociopathy, see D. Black and C. Larson, *Bad Boys, Bad Men: Confronting Antisocial Personality Disorder* (Oxford: Oxford University Press, 2000). See also D. Dutton, with S. Golant, *The Batterer: A Psychological Profile* (New York: Basic Books, 1995); G. Abel, J. Rouleau, and J. Cunningham-Rathner, "Sexually Aggressive Behavior," in *Forensic Psychiatry and Psychology*, eds. J. Curran, A. McGarry, and S. Shah (Philadelphia: F. A. Davis, 1986); L. Grossman and

J. Cavenaugh, "Psychopathology and Denial in Alleged Sex Offenders," *Journal of Nervous and Mental Disease* 178 (1990): 739–744; J. Fox and J. Levin, *Overkill: Mass Murder and Serial Killing Exposed* (New York: Plenum Press, 1994); and R. Simon, *Bad Men Do What Good Men Dream* (Washington, D.C.: American Psychiatric Press, 1996).

page 14 *From nowhere, a line from a thirty-year-old apocalyptic song:* Black Sabbath, "Luke's Wall/War Pigs," *Paranoid*. Warner Bros. Records, 1970.

page 16 *what novelist F. Scott Fitzgerald:* Fitzgerald, *Tender Is the Night.*

Chapter 1. The Seventh Sense

page 27 *In the fourth century, the Christian scholar Saint Jerome:* See G. Evans, *Mediaeval Commentaries on the* Sentences *of Peter Lombard* (Leiden, NY: E. J. Brill, 2002).

page 27 *Jerome's illustrious contemporary, Augustine of Hippo:* See Augustine, *Confessions*, trans. H. Chadwick (Oxford, OH: Oxford Press, 1998), and R. Saarinen, *Weakness of the Will in Medieval Thought from Augustine to Buridan* (Leiden, NY: E. J. Brill, 1994).

page 28 *A solution to the theological dilemma over conscience:* See T. McDermott, ed., *Summa Theologiae: A Concise Translation* (Allen, TX: Thomas More, 1997); B. Kent, "Transitory Vice: Thomas Aquinas on Incontinence," *The Journal of the History of Philosophy* 27 (1989): 199–223; and T. Potts, *Conscience in Medieval Philosophy* (Cambridge: Cambridge University Press, 1980).

page 29 *Freud proposed that in the normal course of development:* See S. Freud, *The Ego and the Id*, in *The Standard Edition of the Complete Psychological Works of Sigmund Freud,* ed. J. Strachey (New York: W. W. Norton, 1990), and S. Freud, *Civilisation and Its Discontents,* in ibid.

Chapter 2. Ice People: The Sociopaths

page 44 *Robert Hare writes:* R. Hare, *Without Conscience*, p. 208.

page 45 *Jane Goodall says the chimpanzees she observed:* J. Goodall, *Through a Window: My Thirty Years with the Chimpanzees of Gombe* (New York: Houghton Mifflin, 2000), pp. 210–211.

Chapter 3. When Normal Conscience Sleeps

page 57 *to borrow an expression from Ervin Staub:* E. Staub, *The Roots of Evil: The Origins of Genocide and Other Group Violence* (Cambridge: Cambridge University Press, 1989). See also E. Staub, "Ethnopolitical and Other Group Violence: Origins and Prevention," in *Ethnopolitical Warfare: Causes, Consequences, and Possible Solutions*, eds. D. Chirot and M. Seligman (Washington, D.C.: American Psychological Association, 2001), and N. Smith, "The Psycho-Cultural Roots of Genocide," *American Psychologist* 53 (1998): 743–753.

page 59 *One explanation is our trancelike state:* For descriptions and examples of dissociative states, see M. Stout, *The Myth of Sanity.* For a discussion of how dissociative phenomena may affect whole populations, see L. deMause, *The Emotional Life of Nations* (New York: Karnac, 2002).

page 60 *In 1961 and 1962, in New Haven, Connecticut:* S. Milgram, "Behavioral Study of Obedience," *Journal of Abnormal and Social Psychology* 67 (1963): 371–378. See also S. Milgram, *Obedience to Authority: An Experimental View* (New York: Perennial, 1983), and T. Blass, ed., *Obedience to Authority: Current Perspectives on the Milgram Paradigm* (Mahwah, NJ: Lawrence Erlbaum Associates, 2000).

page 65 *Brig. Gen. S. L. A. Marshall:* S. Marshall, *Men against Fire: The Problem of Battle Command in Future War* (Gloucester, MA: Peter Smith, 1978), p. 30.

page 66 *In his book* On Killing: D. Grossman, *On Killing: The Psychological Cost of Learning to Kill in War and Society* (Boston: Back Bay Books, 1996), p. xv.

page 66 *As Peter Watson writes:* P. Watson, *War on the Mind: The Military Uses and Abuses of Psychology* (New York: Basic Books, 1978), p. 250.

page 68 *In contrast, research involving Vietnam veterans:* J. Stellman and S. Stellman, "Post Traumatic Stress Disorders among American Legionnaires in Relation to Combat Experience: Associated and Contributing Factors," *Environmental Research* 47 (1988): 175–210. This research, involving 6,810 randomly selected veterans, examined the relationship between symptoms of PTSD and participation in the killing process, and was the first study to quantify levels of combat.

Chapter 4. The Nicest Person in the World

page 76 *Doreen Littlefield is what personality theorist Theodore Millon would call:* Many people have tried to identify different kinds of sociopaths. One of the most interesting typologies is Theodore Millon's. Millon identifies ten subtypes of psychopathy: covetous, unprincipled, disingenuous, risk-taking, spineless, explosive, abrasive, malevolent, tyrannical, and malignant. He notes that "the number 10 is by no means special. . . . Taxonomies may be put forward at levels that are more coarse or more fine-grained." Millon's taxonomy is detailed in T. Millon and R. Davis, "Ten Subtypes of Psychopathy," in *Psychopathy: Antisocial, Criminal, and Violent Behavior,* eds. T. Millon et al.

page 82 *on average only about 20 percent of prison inmates in the United States:* See R. Hare, K. Strachan, and A. Forth, "Psychopathy and Crime: A Review," in *Clinical Approaches to Mentally Disordered Offenders,* eds. K. Howells and C. Hollin (New York: Wiley, 1993), and S. Hart and R. Hare, "Psychopathy: Assessment and

Association with Criminal Conduct," in *Handbook of Antisocial Behavior*, eds. D. Stoff, J. Breiling, and J. Maser (New York: Wiley, 1997).

Chapter 5. Why Conscience Is Partially Blind

page 90 *Relatedly, people without conscience have an uncanny sense:* See L. Robins, *Deviant Children Grown Up: A Sociological and Psychiatric Study of Sociopathic Personality* (Huntington, NY: Krieger Publishing, 1974).

page 93 *Benjamin Wolman:* B. Wolman, *Antisocial Behavior: Personality Disorders from Hostility to Homicide* (Amherst, NY: Prometheus Books, 1999), p. 136.

page 99 *We raise our children, especially girls:* See D. Cox, S. Stabb, and K. Bruckner, *Women's Anger: Clinical and Developmental Perspectives* (Philadelphia: Brunner-Routledge, 1999); L. Brown, *Raising Their Voices: The Politics of Girls' Anger* (Cambridge, MA: Harvard University Press, 1999), p. 166; L. Brown, "Educating the Resistance: Encouraging Girls' Strong Feelings and Critical Voices" (paper presented at the 20th Annual Conference of the Association of Moral Education, Calgary/Banff, Canada, 1994); C. Gilligan, "Women's Psychological Development: Implications for Psychotherapy," *Women and Therapy* 11 (1991): 5–31; and L. Brady, "Gender Differences in Emotional Development: A Review of Theories and Research," *Journal of Personality* 53 (1985): 102–149.

page 100 *As for the boys:* See D. Kindlon and M. Thompson, *Raising Cain: Protecting the Emotional Life of Boys* (New York: Ballantine Books, 2000), p. 99.

Chapter 6. How to Recognize the Remorseless

page 109 *in the 1945 interrogations that preceded the Nuremberg War Crimes Tribunal:* Reported in R. Overy, *Interrogations: The Nazi Elite in Allied Hands, 1945* (New York: Viking Penguin, 2001), p. 373.

Chapter 7. The Etiology of Guiltlessness: What Causes Sociopathy?

page 122 *studies on twins have shown that personality features:* For a detailed discussion of such findings, see L. Eaves, H. Eysenck, and N. Martin, *Genes, Culture and Personality* (New York: Academic Press, 1989).

page 122 *A number of such studies have included the "Psychopathic Deviate" (Pd) scale:* For a review of twin studies that have used the Pd scale, see H. Goldsmith and I. Gottesman, "Heritable Variability and Variable Heritability in Developmental Psychopathology," in *Frontiers in Developmental Psychopathology,* eds. M. Lenzenweger and J. Haugaard (Oxford: Oxford University Press, 1996).

page 123 *In 1995, a major longitudinal study:* M. Lyons et al., "Differential Heritability of Adult and Juvenile Antisocial Traits," *Archives of General Psychiatry* 52 (1995): 906–915.

page 123 *Still other studies have found:* See T. Widiger et al., "A Description of the DSM-III-R and DSM-IV Personality Disorders with the Five-factor Model of Personality," in *Personality Disorders and the Five-factor Model,* eds. P. Costa and T. Widiger (Washington, D.C.: American Psychological Association, 1994), and C. Cloninger, "A Systematic Method for Clinical Description and Classification of Personality Variants," *Archives of General Psychiatry* 44 (1987): 579–588.

page 123 *The Texas Adoption Project:* See L. Willerman, J. Loehlin, and J. Horn, "An Adoption and a Cross-Fostering Study of the Minnesota Multiphasic Personality Inventory (MMPI) Psychopathic Deviate Scale," *Behavior Genetics* 22 (1992): 515–529.

page 123 *a heritability estimate of 54 percent can be derived:* For more on how heritability estimates are derived for psychopathic deviance and other characteristics, see P. McGuffin and A. Thapar, "Genetics and Antisocial Personality Disorder," in *Psychopathy: Antisocial, Criminal, and Violent Behavior,* eds. T. Millon et al., and D.

Falconer, *Introduction to Quantitative Genetics* (Edinburgh: Churchill Livingstone, 1989).

page 124 *Some of the most interesting information about cortical functioning in sociopathy:* See S. Williamson, T. Harpur, and R. Hare, "Abnormal Processing of Affective Words by Psychopaths," *Psychophysiology* 28 (1991): 260–273, and J. Johns and H. Quay, "The Effect of Social Reward on Verbal Conditioning in Psychopathic and Neurotic Military Offenders," *Journal of Consulting and Clinical Psychology* 26 (1962): 217–220.

page 125 *In related research using single-photon emission-computed tomography:* J. Intrator et al., "A Brain Imaging (SPECT) Study of Semantic and Affective Processing in Psychopaths," *Biological Psychiatry* 42 (1997): 96–103.

page 129 *In fact, there is some evidence that sociopaths:* See R. Hare, *Without Conscience.*

page 130 *This arrangement promotes a sense of order and safety:* J. Bowlby, *Attachment and Loss* (New York: Basic Books, 1969).

page 130 *Research tells us that adequate attachment in infancy:* For a discussion of attachment theory, see D. Siegel, *The Developing Mind: How Relationships and the Brain Interact to Shape Who We Are* (New York: Guilford Press, 1999).

page 131 *In 1989, when the Communist regime in Romania fell:* For further discussion of Ceauşescu's reproductive policies, see G. Kligman, *The Politics of Duplicity: Controlling Reproduction in Ceauşescu's Romania* (Berkeley: University of California Press, 1998).

page 132 *And then a couple in Paris would discover:* See P. Pluye et al., "Mental and Behavior Disorders in Children Placed in Long-Term Care Institutions in Hunedoara, Cluj and Timis, Romania," *Santé* 11 (2001): 5–12, and T. O'Connor and M. Rutter, "Attachment Disorder Behavior Following Early Severe Deprivation: Extension and Longitudinal Follow-up. English and Romanian Adoptees Team," *Journal of the American Academy of Child and Adolescent Psychiatry* 39 (2000): 703–712.

page 133 *In Scandinavian child psychiatry:* See M. Lier, M. Gammeltoft, and I. Knudsen, "Early Mother-Child Relationship: The Copenhagen Model of Early Preventive Intervention Towards Mother-Infant Relationship Disturbances," *Arctic Medical Research* 54 (1995): 15–23.

page 135 *As an illustration, psychiatric anthropologist Jane M. Murphy:* J. Murphy, "Psychiatric Labeling in Cross-Cultural Perspective: Similar Kinds of Disturbed Behavior Appear to Be Labeled Abnormal in Diverse Cultures," *Science* 191 (1976): 1019–1028.

page 136 *Intriguingly, sociopathy would appear to be relatively rare in certain East Asian countries:* See P. Cheung, "Adult Psychiatric Epidemiology in China in the 1980s," *Culture, Medicine, and Psychiatry* 15 (1991): 479–496; W. Compton et al., "New Methods in Cross-Cultural Psychiatry: Psychiatric Illness in Taiwan and the United States," *American Journal of Psychiatry* 148 (1991): 1697–1704; H.-G. Hwu, E.-K. Yeh, and L. Change, "Prevalence of Psychiatric Disorders in Taiwan Defined by the Chinese Diagnostic Interview Schedule," *Acta Psychiatrica Scandinavica* 79 (1989): 136–147; and T. Sato and M. Takeichi, "Lifetime Prevalence of Specific Psychiatric Disorders in a General Medicine Clinic," *General Hospital Psychiatry* 15 (1993): 224–233.

page 136 *The 1991 Epidemiologic Catchment Area study:* See L. Robins and D. Regier, eds., *Psychiatric Disorders in America: The Epidemiologic Catchment Area Study* (New York: Free Press, 1991), and R. Kessler et al., "Lifetime and 12-Month Prevalence of DSM-III-R Psychiatric Disorders in the United States," *Archives of General Psychiatry* 51 (1994): 8–19.

page 136 *Robert Hare writes:* R. Hare, *Without Conscience*, p. 177.

page 139 *Sociopaths are fearless and superior warriors:* See D. Grossman, *On Killing*, p. 185.

Chapter 8. The Sociopath Next Door

page 157 *The good news is that having social support:* See T. Blass, ed., *Obedience to Authority: Current Perspectives on the Milgram Paradigm.*

Chapter 9. The Origins of Conscience

page 164 *Since we have it on excellent authority that nature is red in tooth and claw:* A. Tennyson, "In Memorium, A.H.H.," in *Alfred, Lord Tennyson: Selected Poems,* ed. M. Baron (London: Phoenix Press, 2003). It is noteworthy that Tennyson wrote this poem in 1850, nine years before the publication of Darwin's *The Origin of Species.*

page 166 *According to psychobiologist Frans de Waal:* See F. de Waal, *Good Natured: The Origins of Right and Wrong in Humans and Other Animals* (Cambridge, MA: Harvard University Press, 2001), and F. de Waal and P. Tyack, eds, *Animal Social Complexity: Intelligence, Culture, and Individualized Societies* (Cambridge, MA: Harvard University Press, 2003).

page 167 *In 1966, George C. Williams:* G. Williams, *Adaptation and Natural Selection* (Princeton, NJ: Princeton University Press, 1966).

page 168 *And ten years later, in 1976:* R. Dawkins, *The Selfish Gene* (Oxford: Oxford University Press, 1976).

page 168 *biologist W. D. Hamilton's notion:* See W. Hamilton, "Selection of Selfish and Altruistic Behavior," in *Man and Beast: Comparative Social Behavior,* eds. J. Eisenberg and W. Dillon (Washington, D.C.: Smithsonian Institution Press, 1971).

page 170 *Naturalist Gould reexamines the evidence from paleontology:* S. Gould, *The Structure of Evolutionary Theory* (Cambridge, MA: Harvard University Press, 2002).

page 170 *As evolutionist David Sloan Wilson has said:* See D. Wilson and E. Sober, "Reintroducing Group Selection to the Human Behavioral Sciences," *Behavioral and Brain Sciences* 17 (1994): 585–654.

page 172 *Swiss psychologist Jean Piaget:* J. Piaget, *The Moral Judgment of the Child* (New York: Collier Books, 1962).

page 173 *psychologist and educator Lawrence Kohlberg:* L. Kohlberg, *The Philosophy of Moral Development* (New York: Harper & Row, 1981).

page 176 *in 1982, in a groundbreaking book by Carol Gilligan:* C. Gilligan, *In a Different Voice: Psychological Theory and Women's Development* (Cambridge, MA: Harvard University Press, 1982).

page 177 *In the last twenty years, newer studies:* See, for example, J. Walker, "Sex Differences in Moral Reasoning," in *Handbook of Moral Behavior and Development,* eds. W. Kurtines and J. Gewirtz (Hillsdale, NJ: Lawrence Erlbaum Associates, 1991).

page 177 *One illustration of the significance of context and culture:* See J. Miller and D. Bersoff, "Development in the Context of Everyday Family Relationships: Culture, Interpersonal Morality, and Adaptation," in *Morality in Everyday Life: Developmental Perspectives,* eds. M. Killen and D. Hart (Cambridge: Cambridge University Press, 1995), and J. Miller, D. Bersoff, and R. Harwood, "Perceptions of Social Responsibilities in India and in the United States: Moral Imperatives or Personal Decisions?" *Journal of Personality and Social Psychology* 58 (1990): 33–47.

page 178 *An overall perception of good and evil as a duality in human life:* For additional findings and theories concerning this ubiquitous feature of human relations, see J. Crocker and A. Miller, eds., *The Social Psychology of Good and Evil* (New York: Guilford Press, 2004).

Chapter 10. Bernie's Choice: Why Conscience Is Better

page 183 *virtually identical Y chromosomes are carried by almost 8 percent:* T. Zerjal et al., "The Genetic Legacy of the Mongols," *American Journal of Human Genetics* 72 (2003): 717–721.

page 187 *Laboratory experiments using electric shocks and loud noises:* See, for example, J. Ogloff and S. Wong, "Electrodermal and Cardiovascular Evidence of a Coping Response in Psychopaths," *Criminal Justice and Behavior* 17 (1990): 231–245. See also A. Raine and P. Venables, "Skin Conductance Responsivity in Psychopaths to Orienting, Defensive, and Consonant Vowel Stimuli," *Journal of Psychophysiology* 2 (1988), 221–225.

page 187 *A major comorbidity study published in 1990:* D. Regier et al., "Comorbidity of Mental Disorders with Alcohol and Other Drug Abuse: Results from the Epidemiologic Catchment Area Study," *Journal of the American Medical Association* 264 (1990): 2511–2518.

page 187 *Another study, published in 1993:* R. Brooner, L. Greenfield, C. Schmidt, and G. Bigelow, "Antisocial Personality Disorder and HIV Infection Among Intravenous Drug Abusers," *American Journal of Psychiatry* 150 (1993): 53–58.

page 189 *lives in a torment of hypochondriacal reactions:* See Guze, R. Woodruff, and P. Clayton, "Hysteria and Antisocial Behavior: Further Evidence of an Association," *American Journal of Psychiatry* 127 (1971): 957–960, and L. Robins, *Deviant Children Grown Up: A Sociological and Psychiatric Study of Sociopathic Personality.*

page 189 *Perhaps the most famous historical example:* For one account, see L. Heston and R. Heston, *Medical Casebook of Adolf Hitler: His Illnesses, Doctors, and Drugs* (New York: Cooper Square Press, 2000).

page 193 *In a systematic study of such people:* See A. Colby and W. Damon, *Some Do Care: Contemporary Lives of Moral Commitment* (New York: Free Press, 1992), p. 262, and A. Colby and W. Damon, "The Development of Extraordinary Moral Commitment," in *Morality in Everyday Life: Development Perspectives,* eds. M. Killen and D. Hart, p. 364.

Chapter 11. Groundhog Day

page 197 *Tillie is someone personality theorist Theodore Millon would call:* See T. Millon and R. Davis, "Ten Subtypes of Psychopathy," in *Psychopathy: Antisocial, Criminal, and Violent Behavior,* eds. T. Millon et al., and the first note for chapter 4, which concerns Millon's subtypes.

Chapter 12. Conscience in Its Purest Form: Science Votes for Morality

page 212 *Vietnamese Buddhist master Thich Nhat Hanh:* T. Hanh, *Peace Is Every Step: The Path of Mindfulness in Everyday Life* (New York: Bantam Books, 1992).

page 212 *Jewish theologian and philosopher Martin Buber:* M. Buber, *Between Man and Man* (New York: Collier Books, 1965), p. 117.

page 213 *psychologist Daniel Goleman and His Holiness the Dalai Lama:* D. Goleman (Narrator), *Destructive Emotions: A Scientific Dialogue with the Dalai Lama* (New York: Bantam Dell, 2003), p. 12.

page 213 *More specifically, the Dalai Lama said:* Mind and Life Institute, *Investigating the Mind: Exchanges between Buddhism and the Biobehavioral Sciences on How the Mind Works,* sound recording (Berkeley, CA: Conference Recording Service, Inc., 2003).

page 214 *As ways to increase life satisfaction:* See M. Seligman's groundbreaking book on positive psychology, *Authentic Happiness: Using the New Positive Psychology to Realize Your Potential for Lasting Fulfillment* (New York: Free Press, 2002).

page 214 *"The Wise Woman's Stone"*: A version of this parable can be found in A. Lenehan, ed., *The Best of Bits and Pieces* (Fairfield, NJ: Economics Press, 1994), p. 73.

page 216 *Conscience is the still small voice:* I would like to thank the eminent international relations scholar James A. Nathan for pointing out to me (personal communication) that the transliterated Hebrew phrase *kol demama dakah* (that still small voice within) derives from a story about the prophet Elijah, "who experienced fires, earthquakes, and assorted terrors, and then the still small voice of God and conscience."

index

about the author

MARTHA STOUT, Ph.D., was trained at the famous McLean Psychiatric Hospital and is a practicing psychologist and a clinical instructor in the Department of Psychiatry at Harvard Medical School. She is the author of *The Myth of Sanity: Divided Consciousness and the Promise of Awareness* and has been featured on Fox News, National Public Radio, KABC, and many other broadcasts. She lives on Cape Ann, Massachusetts.